"By anticipating what is expected and developing Habits of Achievement, you put yourself in a position to excel and receive even greater opportunities."

James E. McLeod

Habits of Achievement

Lessons for a Life Well-Lived

Herb Weitman

James E. McLeod

Permissions acknowledgments appear on page 76.

ISBN 978-0-9885244-0-8 (hardcover: alk. paper)

CONTENTS

Habits of Achievement

Lessons for a Life Well-Lived

FOREWORD

Habits of Achievement tells the story of one of the great architects of the student experience at Washington University, James Earl McLeod. But it is more than that. It is a reminder of how Jim taught us to treat one another, to be successful and to make our world a better place.

Like many who contributed to this book, I considered Jim to be my friend. He was a source of inspiration and ideas. He was a counselor, and he was an outstanding leader. When I came to Washington University as chancellor in 1995, Jim McLeod already had developed a reputation as a wise and thoughtful senior administrator as dean of the College of Arts & Sciences. I am proud that I asked Jim to take on the dual roles of vice chancellor for students and dean of the College of Arts & Sciences. Washington University in 1995 was a great university, but like all great universities, we knew we could become even better, and I asked a lot of Jim in helping us to become a stronger university. My confidence in Jim proved to be very well-placed, indeed! Students are at the heart of everything we do, and Jim McLeod developed for students an unparalleled academic and co-curricular experience. Jim was the architect of many great improvements — a residential college system that strengthened connections between the

Joe Angeles

Chancellor Mark S. Wrighton

academic and co-curricular life of the campus; an advising system that guided students to become better scholars; a research initiative designed to pique the interest of students early in their studies. The list goes on.

Universities are complicated institutions where progress is often slow and difficult. In developing the undergraduate experience at Washington University, Jim McLeod showed remarkable skill at bringing people together around common ideas. It is hard for all of us to explain Jim's success, but this book reveals some of the secrets behind his methods and his approach.

All who knew Jim understood how proud he was of the John B. Ervin Scholars Program and the many distinguished graduates produced by the program. It was fitting that Jim's "Habits of Achievement" talk was a cornerstone of the Ervin orientation. Jim had tremendous expectations for our Ervin Scholars, and he hoped his message would help guide these scholars toward lives of success and achievement. Jim's message, though, resonates with all of us.

Jim set the tone for how all of us in the Washington University community should live together and learn together. I expect that *Habits of Achievement* will serve as an enduring reminder to those who knew James Earl McLeod about how we should view our responsibilities to ourselves and to others.

—Mark S. Wrighton, Chancellor, 1995–Present

INTRODUCTION

This book, inspired by the life and teachings of Dean James E. McLeod, is for you who want to take on one of the greatest challenges of a lifetime — self-creation, making yourself the best person that you can be. It is about developing habits that make for a strong character; it is about building a character that will guide your decisions, large and small, and thus determine your destiny. This book is not for those who seek an easy life, or for those who hope there will be no need for self-discipline, for setting priorities, or for realizing that the needs of others are as important as your own. Great accomplishments will still require hard work. But those who have prepared this book believe that Jim McLeod's message has great value and should be shared. They believe, as do I, that if more people followed his example, our world would be friendlier and kinder and would work better.

Donald Danforth Plant Science Center

William H. Danforth
Chancellor Emeritus

Jim McLeod made Washington University his home for 37 years. No one was more respected, admired, loved and revered. We all learned from him and tried to be more like him. We leaned on his wisdom and judgment. He touched our lives and made us better people. He taught by example and by words. What he said was important, who he was even more so.

He was intelligent, kind and gentle. He understood us all and helped us build on our strengths and minimize our weaknesses. His friendly smile, warm and welcoming, immediately set others at ease. He was ready to work with and help people of all nationalities, ethnic groups, backgrounds, passions and beliefs. He never seemed hurried or distracted. He gave his full attention to the person in front of him. He was never too busy to help anyone in need.

Jim was honest and truthful, although hard truths were always gently stated. He had a strong sense of right and wrong and the courage to stand by his convictions in the face of heated opposition; but he expressed his views with such kindness, gentleness and respect for others that his words — even those at odds with the cause of the moment — calmed rather than inflamed passions.

He worked hard, very hard, to make Washington University an ideal community of learners and teachers, a place in which each student achieved a first-rate education and was able to make the most of his or her talents, interests and passions. He worked to create a community of mutual respect, a community in which someone knew every student by name and story, a community in which students grew in knowledge and intellect and also in character, in friendships, in understanding of people different from themselves. He wanted people to be both learned and good, to master their studies and understand and value their fellow classmates.

His life was our blessing. I hope this book helps it to be yours as well.

—William H. Danforth, Chancellor Emeritus

About This Book

When James E. McLeod spoke, in his quiet way, he offered words of encouragement, humor, friendship, love — even when it was tough love.

Perhaps the most important group he supported, inspired, encouraged and admonished were Washington University students. Among the students who clearly benefited from his lessons about how to succeed in college and afterward were those in the Ervin Scholars Program.

Beginning in 1991, McLeod, as director of the Ervin Scholars Program, gave a talk to new Ervin Scholars at orientation called "Habits of Achievement." He laced his Habits talk with stories and anecdotes from his own life. Bringing the concept of storytelling full circle, he famously coined the phrase that every student should be known "by name and by story."

McLeod's Habits of Achievement talk resonated with students and went with them when they became alumni. As planning for the 25th anniversary celebration of the Ervin Scholars Program in fall 2012 was underway, some alumni determined they wanted to re-create the Habits of Achievement (which had never been written down) and see it published. The effort, led by Trina (Williams) Shanks, Ervin Class of 1992, worked from recordings of portions of the Habits talk and from personal notes kept by Ervin Scholars.

The thread that runs through the first section of this book (in black type) is the Habits talk. Current Ervin Scholars and Ervin Program alumni tell their own stories (in blue type) of what the Habits of Achievement have meant to them.

Also included are sayings McLeod shared with the incoming students that are related to the habits he advocated — ranging from Alfred Binet to Nelson Mandela. The result is both an inspirational set of life lessons and a tribute to the man who was teacher, mentor, friend and role model.

CULTIVATING HABITS OF ACHIEVEMENT

James E. McLeod

"To me, the most meaningful words Dean McLeod ever said — which I actually hung up on my wall freshman year and had framed and have had up on my wall ever since, no matter where I've lived — are the words he taught us in the Habits of Achievement. Remember who you are, where you come from, where you are going, what you stand for. Those are the hallmarks that I try to define my life by. Every speech and every thing that I do from now on, I will try to impart [Dean McLeod's 'Habits'] because I think those are incredibly wise words."

Fernando Cutz, Class of 2010
Major: International and Area Studies
Currently presidential management fellow at USAID

Introduction

What do you want to be? What does success mean to you? Be ambitious, set goals and dream big! But for the moment, tuck these ideas away. First, you must decide to develop the Habits of Achievement today that will prepare you to perform at the highest levels.

Achievement is "exceptional performance at a point in time." Each performance is usually short and may be predictable (like an exam) or unpredictable (like an impromptu speech or interview). No one performance defines you and there can always be a next time, but in order to consistently achieve exceptional performance, you must be prepared. Preparation requires planning and effort — this is what matters.

Some people think that intelligence or high school reputation or who your friends are is what is most important. These things are already decided, mostly out of your control, and part of the past that brought you to this current situation. In actuality, your attitude — how you position yourself and the effort you are willing to expend — are what will prepare you for exceptional performance and eventually achieving your goals.

As mentioned, dreaming big is good because dreams are inspiring, but setting goals is even more important because they are things you can actually achieve. I used to dream of being an NBA basketball player. Although I practiced when I could and hoped I would grow a bit taller, this dream has not yet become a reality. I can still dream of being an NBA star, but day to day I set and achieve goals relevant to my current position. So think about what you want to be, what success will look like for you, then pursue the goals that will help you reach the future you desire.

Courtesy Ervin Scholars Program

Because Dean McLeod often shared his dream of becoming an NBA basketball star, the Ervin Scholars Class of 2006 gave him his own jersey.

Once you have decided to make the effort to achieve, it is necessary to translate that effort into habits. Habits are essential because they are what we can actually control. More importantly, we become our habits. We live by them; we die by them. The body seeks them, relaxes in them, stresses when they change. So first, know yourself and take stock of your habits. They are you. They limit you. They determine your potential.

> *A few modern philosophers ... assert that an individual's intelligence is a fixed quantity, a quantity which cannot be increased. We must protest and react against this brutal pessimism. ... With practice, training, and above all, method, we manage to increase our attention, our memory, our judgment and literally to become more intelligent than we were before.*
>
> — Alfred Binet, *Modern Ideas About Children, (Les idées modernes sur les enfants)*, 1909

At Ervin Scholars orientation, Dean McLeod shared some of his favorite quotes that were related to the Habits of Achievement.

It is not easy to change a habit. But if there is something in your life that deters you from exceptional performance, it has to go. Decide that you want to achieve badly enough and work on it. Change necessitates a coordination of mind and body, even mind over body. You have to practice. This is not easy — it requires effort and the ability to be aware and control yourself. The good news,

"Dean McLeod often stated how dreams are inspiring, including his own glorious one of becoming an NBA star. To be fair, he occasionally acknowledged the challenges inherent in that pursuit — namely his less-than-appropriate stature. Nonetheless, he held steadfast to the thought of one day achieving that dream.

After sharing this dream for many years, many wondered why the dreamer never practiced his jumpshot. His dream never materialized because he *purposely* selected his life's goals to be something that resonated even deeper with him than proverbial stardom. He cultivated another dream that resonated within him even stronger and thus became his life's goal — impacting the lives of countless minds. This life goal was bolstered by his own Habits of Achievement, which prepared him for each vicissitude or sequential stage of life.

In instructing us how to select goals, he taught that even well-intentioned goals can potentially contain unintended perils. For example, while we were expected to plan big, we 'tucked away' long-term goals to focus intently on each short-term step. Placing each successive life mini-goal just out of immediate reach serves us well and leads us down the path of repeatable achievement."

Jerome Strickland, Class of 2002
Major: African and Afro-American Studies
Currently doing marketing strategy/analytics at Cardinal Health

At times when you're working, you'll sit there feeling hung over and bored, and you may or may not be able to pull yourself up out of it that day. But it is fantasy to think that successful [persons] do not have these bored, defeated hours, these hours of deep insecurity when one feels as small and jumpy as a water bug. They do.

What's real is that if you do your scales every day, if you slowly try harder and harder pieces, if you listen to great musicians play music you love, you'll get better.

— Excerpts from *Bird by Bird: Some Instructions on Writing and Life,* by Anne Lamott

"As a varsity football player, I was able to attend only a couple hours of Ervin fall retreat every year. My sophomore year, after a morning practice, I arrived at a hotel conference room full of Ervin Scholars and sat in the back, relatively unnoticed. I was embarrassed to show up late, having missed out on the activities that had already taken place. Dean McLeod was in the middle of giving his Habits of Achievements lessons and was speaking about his dreams of becoming a professional basketball player. I was not sitting there for more than two minutes when Dean McLeod said that his size was a disadvantage in trying to make the NBA, and how he did not 'have big shoulders like Tim Taylor.' It was a small comment in the scope of the speech, but it meant so much to me, as he showed acknowledgment and appreciation of my presence at retreat and as part of the Ervin family."

Tim Taylor, Class of 2010
Major: Computer Science
Currently a software developer at Morgan Stanley in New York City

"I wouldn't be where I am now without Dean McLeod's influence. I thought about his advice this morning when I started to teach my first class; I thought about his challenges to us when I was planning strategies to learn my students' names early this afternoon, and though it's such a habit now to wear a watch that I didn't think about it when I put it on this morning, I know I'll be thinking about it tomorrow."

Nadia Mann, Class of 2010
Major: International and Area Studies
Currently working on a PhD in Hispanic Languages and Literatures at Boston University and teaching Spanish grammar classes as a Presidential Teaching Fellow

however, is if you force yourself to practice a new habit for three weeks, it becomes your own. The effort pays off, and the new habit that supports your achievement becomes part of your daily (and eventually unconscious) routine.

Preliminary Points

Before sharing a broad set of habits to help prepare you for achievement, you should know a few more preliminary points. First, you need to get organized. One important part of organization is that you must measure and budget your time. Everyone has only 24 hours in a day, so you must keep track of your time and plan the use of it. This requires tools.

Time Budget Sheet

Weekly Time Budget

	Monday	Tuesday	Wednesday	Thursday	Friday	Saturday	Sunday
8:00am							
8:30am							
9:00am							
9:30am							
10:00am							
10:30am							
11:00am							
11:30am							
12:00pm							
12:30pm							
1:00pm							
1:30pm							
2:00pm							
2:30pm							
3:00pm							
3:30pm							
4:00pm							
4:30pm							
5:00pm							
5:30pm							
6:00pm							
6:30pm							
7:00pm							
7:30pm							
8:00pm							
8:30pm							
9:00pm							
9:30pm							
10:00pm							
10:30pm							
11:00pm							
11:30pm							
12:00am							

In his orientation talk, Dean McLeod advised incoming Ervin Scholars to "get organized" and gave them planning tools, such as this "Weekly Time Budget." See Appendix A for more planning tools.

"You must measure and budget your time.... You must keep track of it and plan the use of it.... You need a watch and a calendar.... You need some sort of planner."

Herb Weitman

Professor McLeod shares a lesson with Lee Clark, AB '90, MBA '00.

Measure Your Time

I never used to wear a watch.
I didn't think it was really that important.
Every year at winter retreat Dean McLeod spoke
Of how it looked to others when you wore it —
That their time was important.
I thought it was just something extra.
I had my phone or could ask around.

It took until junior year before I got into the habit.
I went abroad and scheduled meetings.
I was cancelled on and postponed, and I finally understood
That it's not about the watch, really,
It's about respect and value of someone else.
And now I can't live without it.
I didn't understand its importance then —
To play the part of success, you have to first look successful.

It's been four years since I made that change,
And now I feel naked without it.
My life and others are timed around it.
I may be late sometimes, but I feel more secure.

Dean McLeod, to me, is not only the inspiration of his speech,
Or the positive impact of his smile.
More than that, he is the way that I live his habits.
He is the subconscious way that I continue in his legacy,
The whisper in my ear that has become a part of me,
Reminding me that our time is a gift,
And it begins at first with wearing a watch.

Chrystal Okonta, Class of 2010
Major: Biology
Currently working at Washington University
as an undergraduate admissions officer

To keep track of time, you need a watch and a calendar; to plan the use of your time, you need some sort of planner. Plan what you're going to do, how much you're going to do and then measure yourself to make sure you achieved it.

If you have something important that you want to have done, I say assign it to a busy person.

Prior to entering college, how you used your time, most likely, was highly dependent on others. Family, teachers, coaches, supervised activities determined most of your time with only a small part left up to you. If you are a freshman, this year represents a major change in your life. More will be required of you, and you will have an opportunity to decide how to handle each new challenge. You will have the most time you will ever have again. For this one year, you have more time than you need. After this year, you will never again have enough time to get done all the things that you have to do. If you do, you haven't challenged yourself properly; you are just coasting.

Herb Weitman

James E. McLeod first came to Washington University as assistant professor of German.

At every moment of the day you have the opportunity to achieve. You will be required to perform again and again. Do it better than you did it the last time.

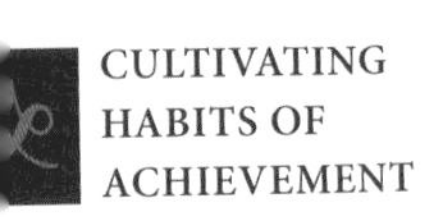

Otherwise you're comfortable, and comfortable equals coasting, which equals slowing down. As you cultivate your own sense of achievement, you must learn to make the most of the time that you have.

If you have something important that you want to have done, I say assign it to a busy person. A busy person who has successfully completed things in the past will know how to control his or her time and will deliver. You can be known as such a dependable person if you just learn to organize your time.

ESE:
E-Eat well
S-Sleep enough
E-Exercise regularly

Second, while a student, you will want to find a place where you can think and study. For most people, this is not your bed or dorm room. You may need to ask around or experiment, but eventually you should have several places where you know you can go to study and prepare for academic performance.

Courtesy Ervin Scholars Program

*Ervin Scholars and others who heard Dean McLeod's orientation talk remember his **E-S-E** advice.*

And lastly, take care of yourself. Again, you are entering a stage where you can no longer depend on others to meet your physical needs. This means taking care of **ESE**. You will need to **E** — eat well (and not too much), **S** — sleep enough (8-10 hours) and **E** — exercise regularly (move every day). It will be hard to sustain exceptional performance if you arepoorly nourished, tired and lack energy.

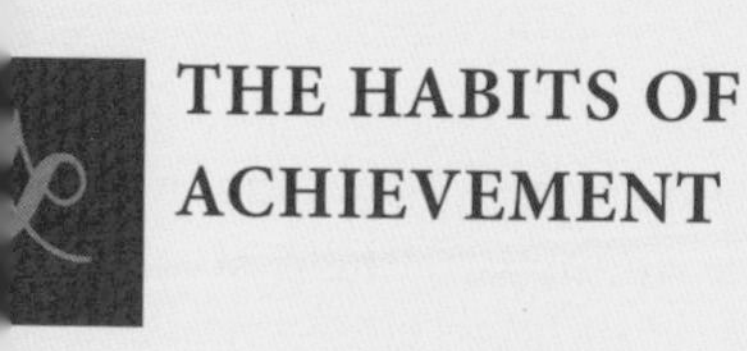

THE HABITS OF ACHIEVEMENT

Watch your thoughts,
they become words.

Watch your words,
they become actions.

Watch your actions,
they become habits.

Watch your habits,
they become character.

Watch your character, for
it becomes your destiny.

— Frank L. Outlaw,
Late president
of BI-LO stores

Opening Thoughts

Habits are a way of approaching life. They are a combination of your beliefs, mindset, attitude and behavior. They are part of your preparation. Anyone considered outstanding in his or her profession has taken years of preparation. As mentioned previously, in order to achieve exceptional performance, you will need to know yourself and cultivate habits that support your goals. What follows is a list of habits that will serve you well. Read them, consider them and slowly find ways to make them your own.

> "Dean McLeod's Habits of Achievement — I think of those on a regular basis, in the work that I do and in discussions I have with my children."
>
> Matt Holton, Class of 1995
> Major: Electrical Engineering
> Currently a senior business leader, Portfolio Management, at MasterCard Worldwide

These are ways of approaching your work, of approaching your life. These are ways of approaching the work that you need to do if you are going to achieve. They're not necessarily things you can work on just today and finish; they're things you should work on for the remainder of your life. They're not things you perfect. They're not things you're going to be able to complete, that you're going to be able to finish.

These are things you work on. You keep your list. And you keep these things before you, to the greatest extent possible, so they remain a guiding light for you.

There's this one quote — how your thoughts become your actions — that is something that has resonated with me. I wish I could know what went on in Dean McLeod's head, because I feel like he just had this amazing mental health, even the way he handled his sickness, the way he handled his busy schedule. He just had to have had this strong mental morale that I admire so much and work each day to achieve. I think part of being an Ervin Scholar and being at this school is working on yourself as a person. I hope the future classes will get that message that he so much ingrained in me.

Bailey Davidson, Class of 2012
Major: Psychology
Currently working as a project manager at Epic, a company that makes electronic medical record software

...in order to achieve exceptional performance, you will need to know yourself and cultivate habits that support your goals.

Joe Angeles

Ervin Scholars discuss recent events with Dean McLeod in 2007. (left to right) Amanda Little ('09), Kimberly Short ('09), Amir Francois ('08), Valerie Wade ('08), McLeod, Fernando Cutz ('10) and Sylvia Lee ('09).

Habit Lesson 1:
Anticipate what is expected.

The more you can anticipate what will come, the better you can prepare and the more likely you are to achieve your goal.

It is important always to know what is coming, so you can prepare appropriately and be ready to achieve high-level performance. You may wonder how this is possible. In sports, you can watch game film and practice how to respond when predictable plays occur. In a class, you can review the syllabus to see what topics will be covered and what assignments will be coming. You also can look at past exams to get a sense of the types of questions that might be asked. You can talk to other students or people who have already accomplished what you hope to achieve. The more you can anticipate what will come, the better you can prepare and the more likely you are to achieve your goal.

Anticipation is two-way. As you perform, people will begin to anticipate who you are and what you are capable of doing. What do your habits reveal? What can others anticipate from you? Your reputation is valuable and hard to change when you don't give your best. By anticipating what is expected and developing Habits of Achievement, you put yourself in a position to excel and receive even greater opportunities.

"I remember the day I first set foot on the Washington U. campus as an Ervin finalist. I immediately fell in love with the campus and people around me whom I met. I was somewhat nervous simply because everyone seemed to be so exceptional.

After getting to know everyone on the first night, we went to sleep (probably later than we should have; Habits of Achievement lesson one) and set the alarm clock to wake us up for our Ervin breakfast with Dean McLeod the next morning, at 8:30 a.m. When I woke up and the clock said 8:45, I almost cried. Along with two other finalists in the suite, I threw on my clothes and we ran down to Wohl as fast as we could. We could hear Dean McLeod just wrapping up his first talk to the rest of the scholars. We stood there, afraid to walk through the door, sure that our names would immediately be crossed off the list. I will never forget the calming smile Dean McLeod had as he shook my hand when I entered the room, already stumbling to get the apology out of my mouth. All he said was, 'It's OK … don't worry, these things happen.'"

Vincent Caesar, Class of 2005
Major: Architecture
Currently working as an architectural designer with Model Edge Design, LLC

"To be honest, I never did master Dean McLeod's Habits of Achievement, though it hasn't been for lack of trying in the past 20-plus years. I just never thought it was worth the effort of trying to conjure up his wryly delivered anecdotes or to remember one of his sage aphorisms. Instead, when I wanted his input on a personal challenge or professional dilemma, I simply picked up the phone and talked to him.

It wasn't so much Dean McLeod's words that supported, comforted and buoyed me all these years, it was his actions — his willingness to be available and accessible long after the Commencement festivities had ended, his own embodiment of the habits and practices that he worked so faithfully to instill in us. That's the memory that sustains me as I continue to struggle with and strive toward the Habits of Achievement that he championed."

Lynnell Thomas, Class of 1993
Major: English Literature and African and Afro-American Studies
Currently associate professor of American studies, UMass Boston

Habit Lesson 2: Strive for self-knowledge and self-management.

Who am I? What do I stand for? Where am I going? Become a student of yourself. If you know yourself, you can challenge yourself and you can find the people to challenge you. This is particularly important right now, because you're in an excellent position to get to know yourself better. If you're a first-year student, you're entering a new community. If you're a senior, you'll be entering a new community next year. If you're a sophomore or junior, you'll be entering a new situation. Each time you enter a new situation or encounter a new challenge, it's an opportunity to know yourself. You go into a new job, you deal with a new set of employees, a new set of bosses, a new set of knuckleheads, and all of a sudden you get to know something about yourself. So it's a particularly good time to go through the questions of self-knowledge. That is: Who am I? How do I respond to all these circumstances?

Joe Angeles

The Ervin Scholars Program staff celebrates 20 years of the program in 2007: (left to right) Adrienne Glore, associate dean of students; James McLeod, program director; Laura Stephenson, assistant director; Vincent Caesar ('05), admissions officer; and Dorothy Elliott, alumni director.

The second part is self-management, which in some ways is very closely related to self-knowledge. Self-management is probably more difficult than self-knowledge. We may simply forget to focus on self-knowledge, but it's hard to manage yourself. Because we're human beings, we have emotions: We love, we try not to hate. We like. We dislike. And it's very difficult to manage all those emotions while we're trying to be rational human beings.

Living with a Roommate

1. If you open it, close it.
2. If you turn it on, turn it off.
3. If you unlock it, lock it up.
4. If you break it, admit it.
5. If you can't fix it, call in someone who can.
6. If you borrow it, return it.
7. If you value it, take care of it.
8. If you make a mess, clean it up.
9. If you move it, put it back.
10. If it belongs to someone else, get permission to use it.
11. If you don't know how to operate it, leave it alone.
12. If it's none of your business, don't ask questions.

— Miriam Hamilton Keare, *"Golden Rules for Living"*

My approach is that I've given up on managing other people, and I just focus on managing myself. I found that's a whole lot better. When I got married, I tried to manage my wife. That was a hopeless case. When I got colleagues to work with, I started by trying to manage them, but it didn't work. They were more energetic, smarter, had better ideas. So I learned to listen rather than to manage them.

I recommend to you, work on managing yourself. Give up on managing your roommate. Give up on managing those people who are special to you. They will be OK. They won't be like you, but they'll be OK.

Set your own standards. It's not what's wrong with the world, it's what you can do with the world. And once you have set a standard, don't allow others to drag you down. People get complacent. Your friends are nice; your mother adores you — but you know better. Don't lower your standards by failing to look at things objectively.

Control yourself, and don't let emotions get the best of you. If you recognize fear, deal with it before it turns into anxiety. If you notice that you are becoming angry, calm down before it leads to violence. If you are given freedom, use it for growth and independence.

I still recall the time when my wife and I welcomed our daughter, Sara. This was 1986, and it was a very happy time. Maybe three to five years after that, she learned how to push my buttons. This is something my daughter still does, even though she's in her 20s — pushes my buttons. Now I thought I was a calm guy. Nothing she said was going to bother me. Nothing she did would faze me whatsoever.

Well, I was wrong. I never wanted to commit homicide as much as on some of those nights when she didn't want to do what I knew she must do. That was a new part of me, which I didn't know about. I didn't understand I could get that angry. I understood I should get to the first story of a building, so I wouldn't throw her out the window. It's very important to have two parents, so one can keep the other from throwing the child out.

One of my favorite memories of Dean McLeod is of running into him randomly at 2:00 o'clock in the afternoon, and his greeting me with 'Good morning, Keri!'

I was taken aback, and I asked him, 'Dean McLeod, it's 2:00 in the afternoon. What's going on?'

And he said to me, 'You know, I didn't like the way my day was going, so I just decided to start it over.' He had the expectation and the perseverance to do something until he got it right. So if that meant starting his day over at 2:00 o'clock in the afternoon, he would do it.

Keri McWilliams, Class of 2001
Major: Communication Design
Currently an attorney with the Minneapolis-based firm of Fredrikson & Byron

Mary Butkus

Women's softball made its debut as a varsity sport at Washington University in spring 2000 and won first place in the University Athletic Association; the inaugural team included Ervin Scholar Keri McWilliams ('01), second from left.

Each new opportunity is a chance to know yourself, and when that happens you should take stock of it. I have learned from my daughter what anger is like, how angry I can get. And that has helped me in my work. I know now I can just go to my desk, go to my office, close the door, take a deep breath and not say what I was going to say.

Challenge yourself. Be willing to try new things. Do you really like your current hobbies, routines and entertainment? Why? Why not? Stretch yourself. Now is the time to risk. You have nothing to lose and might discover joys and delights that you could never have imagined.

Challenge yourself at every turn. You know when you're taking the easy way out. You know when you've got the simpler path that you've chosen. Many students that I speak with are interested in the easy course. We have a number of math courses; the students will say, "Don't take that one, it's harder. Take an easier one."

Someone will say, "Oh, that's enough physics; engineers only need to take this level."

"Oh, you don't need to do a project for that course."

Challenge yourself at every turn. If today you can walk five miles, tomorrow you can walk six. If you continue to challenge yourself, you will know yourself better. You know when something is a challenge.

Now don't be stupid and overdo it. I see some people working out in the gym three

"Freshman year, I met with Dean McLeod and Dean Margaret West regarding the time budget and things like that. Dean McLeod asked me what I expected to get in all my classes. I had Gen[eral] Chemistry. I'd heard how the mean last year was 34 percent, so I said, 'Yeah, I just want to get a B.'

He said, 'Why not an A?'

It had never occurred to me I could actually get an A in a class at Washington U. Pursue for perfection — that was one of the main things he taught me. Even though I don't have straight A's, I definitely always strive for that."

Anthony Maltbia, Class of 2014
Major: Biology

and four hours a day, or spending all night in the library. That's not challenging yourself, that's wearing yourself out.

Create a rich inner life. And no one in this room really knows fully how to do it; each will do it in his or her own way. I think many of you are really into music — music you listen to, that speaks to you. If all you listen to is Beethoven, then that is not enough. Don't listen to just one kind of music. Don't read one kind of book, talk to just one kind of person, take one kind of class, go to one kind of movie. Do something *weird* occasionally. Talk to *weird* people. Go to *weird* places. Do *weird* things. No one is going to hold it against you! You're a college student. This is the last time you'll be able to get away with it. Now there are limits. You know what the limits are. The limits are 1) something that is illegal and 2) is in bad taste.

Courtesy Ervin Scholars Program

(front to back) Ervin Scholars Shelby Carpenter, Maryse Pearce and Kayla Brinkley, all Class of 2010, canoe together at the 2006 Ervin orientation.

Do something different, and do it regularly. We like to do the same things. We like to hang out with the same kind of people. We like to read the same kind of books, listen to the same kind of radio, watch the same kind of television. A rich inner life requires a myriad of experiences. Do something different every day.

The most important part of getting a rich inner life is being alone. It's very helpful to be alone with yourself — take a few minutes alone every day — no phone, no music. Don't do anything; be still. By learning to know yourself and taking time to be mindful of your thoughts and actions, you create a space for reflection and growth.

This is the most difficult part about college life. You just cannot be alone. There's always someone in your room, there's always someone down the hall, always something to do. There's always something open. It's up to you to say "enough," to pull yourself apart and be alone. Now there's a spiritual dimension to that, and I suggest you seek it. You can do it through reading, through meditation, through congregation with others. But one thing you must do is be alone, every day.

"When I think about it, I think college was the first time I was ever aware of myself becoming who I would be. It was the first time I was old enough and observant enough to know that I was changing and developing and becoming this grown-up person. Dean McLeod was always there, and he knew things about me that I didn't know.

So he would encourage me and introduce new ideas. He's the first one who suggested repeatedly, from the time I was a freshman, that I go to graduate school, which I did. He's the one who suggested I consider teaching and scholarship, which I've done. He was sort of an eye in the storm of the tempestuous drama that is being 20.

A couple of years ago, I finished my PhD in history, the History of Gender and Sexuality, and now I'm teaching middle-school social studies. I'm getting some middle-school teaching experience so I can go on to do teacher training and policy work."

N'Jai-An Patters, Class of 2001
Major: Political Science
Currently teaching middle-school social studies

Habit Lesson 3:
Claim ownership.

Whatever you choose to do, first participate, then engage and then commit.

Ownership is another habit that's very difficult for college students. You've been through 18- to 20-plus years living in someone else's space: Your elementary school was not yours; your middle school was not yours; your high school was not yours. Your home was only partially yours. You come to college — someone else's space — and all you have is a little room. Now you have to create a sense of ownership, forgetting all that business of it's not yours. Claim it. Wherever you are, whatever you're doing, with whomever it is, own it.

Bill Stover

Ervin Scholar and Student Union President Michelle Purdy (standing left) and Chancellor Mark S. Wrighton (third from left) welcome town hall participants and members of the audience to the university's Field House on Oct. 8, 2000, for the nationally televised Presidential Debate between Texas Gov. George W. Bush and Vice President Al Gore.

"Dean McLeod knew our stories, our challenges and our dreams. He never stopped teaching. For Ervin Scholars, he imparted that one must take ownership of their Washington University experience, that success and achievement are *not* the same, and that we must cultivate Habits of Achievement. Moreover he inspired each of us to exceed what we believed to be our own expectations."

Michelle A. Purdy, Class of 2001; MA in History 2003
Major: Educational Studies and African and African-American Studies
Currently assistant professor, Department of Teacher Education, Michigan State University

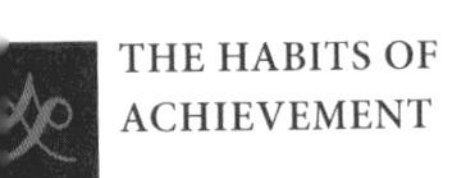

I tell the story of my father who always had a nice car; he always liked his car to be washed, full of gas, oil changed, ready to go. And when I learned to drive, he let me drive his car. I never put any gas in it, never washed it, never waxed it. I drove it, handed him the key and went about my business.

Then, my first year in graduate school I got a '56 Chevy. I tell you that is sweetness. It was rusted all along the bottom panels, everywhere,

Courtesy photo

Ownership: James McLeod poses at San Luis Pass on Galveston Island with George Camp (right), his best friend from graduate school at Rice University, who owned the car behind them. McLeod also owned his first car as a graduate student.

but the rest of it was brilliant shining black wax. It was white on black, and it was terrific. It was *my* car. I owned it. It was always full of gas; the oil was changed. I couldn't afford new tires, so I had retreads.

"In the early days of the Habits of Achievement lessons at the Ervin orientation retreat, Dean McLeod asked us to go to the wall. We reached and we reached and we reached and then marked with a piece of paper how far we were able to reach on the wall. We went about the weekend, then as we came back together, in his fashion he brought it all home as planned.

He asked us to go back to the place on the wall where we marked our reach and challenged us. He said, 'In this moment and in this time you feel this is the extent of your reach, the extent of your power, the extent of what you think you can achieve.' The Ervin Program's expectation and his expectation for us was that we really stretch ourselves while we're at the university, stretch ourselves while we're on campus, stretch ourselves in our leadership, in what we contributed back to campus — to really go beyond what we thought we'd be able to do, to go beyond that little mark on the wall, which at the time seemed as much as we could do."

Amoretta Morris, Class of 1999
Major: Economics
Currently director of attendance for the DC Public Schools

But own whatever you're doing, *own* it. If you're in a class, own the class. It's not the professor's class, it's yours. And ownership means, if it's not going well, you knock on the professor's door. "You know I didn't understand that today, it wasn't very clear to me, could you give me a little clarification on this and that?" Now don't bother the person; if you don't know what you're talking about, don't do it. Do your homework first. Prepare. Anticipate the question before you get to the class. Then let the professor know something wasn't very clear. If it's not a very well-run class, say so.

Another part of ownership is knowing your place. You've come to St. Louis. Most of you here are not from St. Louis; most of you know very little about St. Louis. You can own St. Louis by knowing St. Louis; that's how you own a place. I like to walk in St. Louis, because you see things you can't see otherwise. I like to drive different ways to the same destination, because you get to know the city better. It's a way you know your place and

I remember when Dean McLeod would be on his way to meetings, walking out of Brookings, and I'd tell him I wanted to talk with him. I would ask if I could walk him to his meeting and would start walking toward Graham Chapel. To my surprise, he would always insist we stop right there and talk. He would be completely engaged in the conversation. It often felt like the world stopped for those moments, and it reminded me of how important I was (we all were) to him. He often demonstrated the significant value he placed on personal relationships. I would even claim responsibility for causing many of his tardy meeting arrivals, but each delayed arrival left a timeless mark on who I was as a maturing young man. For that, I am grateful.

Jerome Strickland, Class of 2002
Major: African and Afro-American Studies
Currently doing marketing strategy/analytics at Cardinal Health

> a way you own your place. You're at Washington University, so you ought to know what Washington University is like. You ought to know what your school is like. How do you get to know people? You knock on their door. "Hi, my name is Alison. I wanted to get to know you." They may think you're weird in the beginning, but they won't after a while.

Relationships are the most difficult part of ownership because I would really very much like to manage and control people. I think it's the holy grail of every manager; they want to control people, to tell them what to do, to make them do something. I hope you don't go through my journey with wanting to control people.

WUSTL Photo

Dean McLeod (front) and Chancellor Wrighton (behind him, left) preside over the Residential College Olympics.

The one thing I can tell you about relationships is: I adopt a 100 percent approach to them. Most people think a relationship with another person is 50-50. There's no such thing as 50-50 in a relationship. You'll see this with your roommates. You'll see this in other ways, that one person is responsible for a portion, and another person is responsible for a portion. And then you will say, "Well, I'm not going to budge until that person does his or her part." My advice to you is to take 100 percent responsibility for the nature and the course of the relationship. A number of times I give the example that my wife and I have been married a few years, and she is frequently wrong. I am well aware of that. She is not. But I consider myself 100 percent responsible for maintaining a functioning, calm, reasonable relationship.

In terms of ownership of organizations and events and that sort of thing, participate, engage, commit. Most people in organizations like to lean back, fold their arms, hang back, listen and see how things are going to go. They don't fully engage, they don't fully participate and they rarely commit. We are in a period where it seems important to do lots of things. My advice is to do few things. Do those things you're going to fully participate in, fully engage in, fully commit to.

In my many memories of Dean McLeod, the one that makes me smile is a weekly image of him from my vantage point seated on Sunday mornings in the old St. Louis Bread Company on Delmar Boulevard. He was a proud father who was walking sometimes just ahead of or side by side with his adorable little girl, donning her Sunday best. Although Sara could have been no older than 5 or 6, she kept up with him, perhaps not only in walking pace, but, I suspect, also in conversation. I imagine him making space for her little feet to catch up to his and making room for her to share her deep thoughts and concerns.

I imagine this to be the case because that is what Dean McLeod seemed to do for all who knew him. He made space in his life, space in that wilderness called his office, and space in his heart for everyone. He did so with such grace and ease that you almost forgot that this was a person with many places to be, many things to attend to and many other people tugging at his shirtsleeve. Dean McLeod taught me many things about being confident and brave in the face of fear, encouraged me to stretch beyond my comfort zone and inspired me to continue to set higher and bigger goals in my life. Perhaps the most important lesson he taught me was taught by example — remember to be *present*, which he was with everyone who sought him out.

After leaving Washington University, and with Dean McLeod's support and encouragement, I earned my PhD in psychology from the University of Michigan (1997) and my JD from the University of Pennsylvania (2000).

Sacha Coupet, Class of 1991
Major: Psychology and French
Currently associate professor of law, Loyola University Chicago School of Law

"Dean McLeod's care and assistance continued even once I graduated and left Washington University. We saw one another less frequently, but he still asked how I was, listened carefully, gave his best advice and connected me with people he felt might be helpful. He encouraged my efforts, yet had suggestions for ways I could improve. Paths that came through and from Dean McLeod continually crossed. Sometimes out of the blue, I would receive a note or email saying that Dean McLeod had suggested that I needed to meet with someone; out of respect for him, we would find time to schedule an introduction. I have met several wonderful acquaintances this way.

Dean McLeod was one of the first people to congratulate me when I earned tenure and probably informed many people who knew me on campus of the news. At this point, I was 40 years old and had graduated from Washington University nearly 20 years ago. Yet he still cared and remained engaged."

Trina (Williams) Shanks
Class of 1992; MSW in Social Work 2000; PhD in Social Work 2003
Major: Business Administration
Currently associate professor, School of Social Work, University of Michigan

That's ownership. If you're not going to do that, don't do it. Just don't go, because it's not worth your time. You might as well take a nap. You might as well stare at the trees. You're not getting anything from it, and no one is getting anything from you.

Know your place. Own your place. Wherever you are, make it better. Whatever you choose to do, first participate, then engage and then commit.

Sid Hastings

Kimberly Short ('09) addresses Ervin Scholars and guests at the program's 25th anniversary celebration gala in September 2012.

Whether a class, a project or a community, treat it as if it were all yours. Once you decide "This is mine," you will show your devotion.

I remember wanting to do things on campus that I thought would make the place better, whether that was environmentally or putting together a social event. If we couldn't quite find the right people to help us, we'd call Dean McLeod, and he'd put a call in to the Office of Student Activities and let them know we should find funding for this project. If I wanted to go overseas and go to a UN Conference because I thought it would help my education, he told me to go talk to the Environmental Studies Program, and they would find funding for me. He wanted *everyone* to accomplish their dreams, and he wanted everyone to hold themselves to the highest standards. There was no way he was going to let anything — whether that be funding or time or any other limitation — get in the way of accomplishing that.

Kelley Greenman, Class of 2009
Major: Environmental Studies
Recently completed her efforts as the associate policy director for energy and environment on President Obama's reelection campaign

Own whatever you're doing, *own* it. If you're in a class, own the class. It's not the professor's class, it's yours.

Joe Angeles

Chancellor Mark Wrighton gives Ervin Scholar Kelley Greenman (right) the good news that she has been awarded a prestigious 2008 Harry S. Truman Scholarship, based on her academic performance, leadership and dedication to public service. Looking on is Joy Kiefer, PhD, assistant dean in Arts & Sciences, who nominated Greenman for the award.

Habit Lesson 4: Pursue mastery.

Mastery is an elusive concept. You know it when you see it. Great professional sports persons understand what mastery is; they have measures for those things. One of the great shortstops, Ozzie Smith, was a master at that position. But it's difficult to gauge outside of that context, outside of a professional sports team. How do you master something?

The skill needed for mastery is approach. It's an attitude: I will master this. I may never completely master it, but each time I will get better and better at it. There is simply the next best effort. There is no such thing as failure, because failure is part of learning. If you don't fail, you don't learn. Failing and not recognizing you failed is even worse.

"From the first moment that we had the opportunity to meet our Ervin family, Dean McLeod introduced us to the philosophy of knowing everyone by name and story. His methods of doing so were simple. Every year at Ervin orientation, he would offer $20 to the first person who could name each person in the room by their first and last name — students in their own class, upperclassmen attending orientation, Ervin staff, alumni — truly everyone in the room.

As the Ervin classes grew larger, many of us would stand in front of the room of more than 100 attendees and try our hardest to remember each person's name — from the multiple Jessicas to the many-syllable last names. Only a few succeeded, but many tried, and that effort in itself was pleasing to Dean McLeod. To … those of us who participated, ensuring that we knew someone's first and last name was the genesis of learning their story and building the community that is our Ervin family."

Kimberly Short, Class of 2009
Major: English Literature
Currently a public affairs coordinator at the American Public Health Association in Washington, DC

After my freshman Ervin orientation, I made it my goal to win the 'name game' competition the following year. In Fall 2010, as soon as Dean McLeod asked for volunteers to play the game, my hand shot up. That year, with the help of Lauren Bryant, Class of 2012, I successfully named the approximately 125 Ervins that crowded the Drury Inn meeting room. Needless to say, I was pleasantly surprised when Dean McLeod handed me a crisp $100 bill, which I waved around for the remainder of orientation.

Not until my senior year did I realize the 'competition' was anything but; Dean McLeod's goal was to ensure that we all made the strongest effort to get to know our fellow Ervins; the money was just a bonus. So when the challenge was posed to us during Fall 2012 orientation, just like two years prior, my hand immediately shot up. This time, the reward came from knowing that I was able to help keep one of Dean McLeod's goals alive.

Allory Relf, Class of 2013
Major: Environmental Studies

Mastery is essential to achievement.

Joe Angeles

Dean McLeod takes part in the 2011 Commencement ceremony.

When you master something, you become immersed in it. When you are part of a place, you must understand the whole organization. Just as the seasoned actor knows all the parts of the play, you must master the things for which you are responsible. It isn't about thrill or winning, but about knowing that you have mastered the material.

A good test is whether you can explain it to someone else. If you can't explain it, you don't know it. In class, this means doing your homework. In other areas, it means gathering the relevant information. Become a student everywhere.

"Dean McLeod shared with us a chart of Washington University's organizational structure. He suggested that if we were to be leaders within the university, we had to understand how it works. He walked us step by step through all of the layers of administration and which office was responsible for what. Although I am now a tenured faculty member at another institution, I probably know Washington University as well as or better than my current university."

Trina (Williams) Shanks, Class of 1992; MSW in Social Work 2000; PhD in Social Work 2003
Major: Business Administration
Currently associate professor, School of Social Work, University of Michigan

Take a few things to commit to in good and bad times. Whether it is a technical skill, a spiritual practice or lifelong learning, find a few things that you can master. This might mean finding extra time in your day on top of classes and other requirements. Why would you take it easy? Mastery is essential to achievement.

Winning isn't everything, but mastery is. These twin drives — competition and mastery — are opposite poles. [A person] who relies purely on competitive drive is outward-focused, spurred on by the cheers, glamour, and winning. The problem is, competition-driven persons often lose confidence and tenacity when the going gets rough and others get hostile. They don't know how to get out of a losing streak, because their ego and emotions are timed to winning.

Mastery-oriented persons, by contrast, are driven by internal satisfactions. They pursue an activity with the idea of learning, which they achieve by setting short-term, realistic goals. Instead of blaming themselves (or someone else) for failure, they analyze what they did wrong and address it. By fixating on winning, one often ignores the skills needed for mastery ...

— Madeline Drexler, Boston-based journalist, "Mind and Body: Candidate for Therapy," *The Boston Globe*, Oct. 25, 1992

One of my great experiences with Dean McLeod was freshman year, second semester. I was taking a philosophy class, and I got a C- on my first paper. I felt unfairly graded by the Teaching Assistant, so I took the paper to Dean McLeod, and I expected him to say something about it, do something about it. 'Dean McLeod, this guy is treating me unfairly.'

He looked at me, he looked at my paper for a second, and he just laughed and said, 'He's done you a great favor.'

And I remember being so confused. How could he say the TA had done me a great favor? But Dean McLeod told me, 'If somebody told you your work isn't good enough, it's just somebody telling you that you have room to improve.' And he said, 'From now on, I'd like to read everything you write.'

Solomon Brown, Class of 2014
Major: Political Science and International Business

Sid Hastings

Ervin Scholars from the Class of 2015 gather for a class photo at the program's 25th anniversary celebration in September 2012.

Habit Lesson 5:
Pay attention.

It is getting harder to pay attention because there is so much more stuff to pay attention to. We are programmed to pay attention to certain things. We tend to pay more attention to the negative. You must override your attention to some things and choose to pay attention where it's needed. You can sustain your attention much longer if you take breaks. Every 20 minutes take a two-minute break.

In order to pay attention, you have to pull yourself out of some things in order to point your attention to other things. This means you have to select, and that can be difficult. For example, there's a concept of paying attention, or focus, which is called bottom up. For example, if you were to walk out of this hotel and walk out into the street, you would pay attention to the cars, because they are quite different. Traffic is moving fast, and it's different from the ambience and activity inside. But then there's the other kind of attention where you control what you pay attention to. And it's very difficult to control

Everyone knows what attention is. It is the taking possession by the mind, in clear and vivid form, of one out of what seem several simultaneously possible objects or trains of thought. Focalization, concentration, of consciousness are of its essence. It implies withdrawal from some things in order to deal effectively with others. ...

— William James, *The Principles of Psychology*, 1890

David Kilper

Professor McLeod speaks in Graham Chapel on German Day, 1987.

your focus. Part of it is selecting. The other part of it is suppressing some other things.

Now again in a college context, this can be very difficult. You have friends, lots of things are going on in the hall, in your apartment. Everybody is sitting on your bed. Day and night, lots of things are going on. How can you pay attention and how can you focus? If you can't focus, you can't achieve. If you cannot have exceptional focus, you cannot perform at an exceptional level.

Now, there are a number of ways to do it. First of all, you can avoid certain people. You know who they are: They're always diverting your attention. Your friends? You like them, you should spend time with them — but not always. At your discretion, you set up a time to do that. There's a time for everything. And sometimes there's a time to focus, and then there's a time not to focus, to just let yourself go and enjoy it. Focus is very difficult, but extremely important, not just for learning but also for broader things.

Ecclesiastes 3

There is a time for everything, and a season for every activity under heaven:

A time to be born and a time to die, a time to plant and a time to uproot,

A time to kill and a time to heal, a time to tear down and a time to build,

A time to weep and a time to laugh, a time to mourn and a time to dance,

A time to scatter stones and a time to gather them, a time to embrace and a time to refrain,

A time to search and a time to give up, a time to keep and a time to throw away,

A time to tear and a time to mend, a time to be silent and a time to speak,

A time to love and a time to hate, a time for war and a time for peace.

We're in a period of our history where we are focusing on negative feelings. They're everywhere. They're so thick in this room, you can actually see them. What you experience depends on what you focus on. There are an untold number of things to focus on, to pay attention to; what you choose will determine what happens to you. If you have a roommate who's a very negative person, change roommates. If you have a friend who's always criticizing you — finding something wrong with what you're wearing, talking about, looking at — unfriend the person.

"[Attention] is taking possession of the mind. ...You can be absent or present."

Focusing on the positive, on kindness and hope truly expands your world. Focusing on the negative shrinks your world.

"After my dad's death a week before my 21st birthday, I so wanted to throw in the towel with regard to my education. Nothing felt worth it any more. Thanks to Dean McLeod's encouragement and inspiration, I instead spent that semester completing my Honors thesis and applying to PhD programs. In May 2009, I graduated *magna cum laude* from the College of Arts & Sciences, against all odds. It is still the accomplishment of which I'm most proud in my life.

Today, I'm a year away from finishing my Master of Education in School Counseling. I can't wait to follow in Dean McLeod's footsteps as an educator and, hopefully, to make a fraction of the difference in the lives of my students that he made in mine. I've been happily married for a year now. With my husband, I bought my family home when my mom moved out of it this summer. I'm more stable — emotionally, geographically, financially and in every other way — than I had ever expected to be at 24. I know that every bit of this is a tribute to a remarkable man who always pushed me to be better, to attempt the seemingly impossible, to make more of myself and to give back."

Mackenzie (Leonard) Lober, Class of 2009
Major: Psychology
Currently raising a family after completing her Master's degree

Focusing on upbeat emotions such as hope and kindness literally, not just figuratively, expands your world, just as dwelling on negative feelings shrinks it.

— Barbara L. Fredrickson, PhD, the Kenan Distinguished Professor of Psychology, UNC Chapel Hill

Habit Lesson 6:
Be a giver.

Always find a way to give back — to your family, to a community, to society. Up to this point in your life, many have given to you. As you continue to grow and develop your abilities, find ways to share with others. You can start with small acts of service, helping to meet the needs of someone else. Over time, you will find ways to make a contribution, whether to the campus, organizations, the wider community or your loved ones.

Sid Hastings

Since 1999, Service First has been a signature community service program for first-year students — a daylong event over Labor Day weekend when faculty and staff join student volunteers to brighten public schools for students in St. Louis city, University City and at KIPP: Inspire Academy. Dean McLeod was vice chancellor for students when Service First began.

I live in Oakland, Calif., and am an engineer with the Clorox Company. When I first moved out here, I was pretty much just working because I didn't know anyone. I was really self-involved. I thought about what was missing from college and the Ervin experience, and it was the aspect of service and mentorship. So with a co-worker, I started the Scientific Education Network where we go into schools in the Bay Area and talk about being an engineer and the importance of math and science starting in 4th, 5th, 6th grade all the way up through high school. We've organized this network of people at our job who are really passionate about education and getting kids involved in science and using that to really make a difference in a child's life. I know I wouldn't be doing what I'm doing if someone hadn't done that for me.

Amy Fletcher, Class of 2010
Major: Chemical Engineering
Currently an engineer with Clorox Company

"My favorite time with Dean McLeod was when we three McLeod Scholars took him and Mrs. McLeod out to dinner. He was saying that one of the Ervin alumni asked him, 'After teaching for so long, do things really change?' And he said, 'Yes, something happens every year, and some of my students are taking me out to dinner tonight, which is the first time that's ever happened.' He was so thankful for something as small as us taking him out to dinner."

Michele Hall, Class of 2014
Major: Political Science and African and African-American Studies

At times, you will feel like you are too busy to give. That is when you should fully commit to this habit. You will always *be* more and *receive* more when you find ways to give to others.

Do all the good you can,
By all the means you can,
In all the ways you can,
In all the places you can,
To all the people you can,
As long as ever you can.

— John Wesley

Sid Hastings

The James E. McLeod Scholars gather at a luncheon in their honor at the Chancellor's residence on January 16, 2013. They are (left to right) Front row: Isabel Gloria ('15), Ana Solorio ('14), Vivian Zhu ('15). Middle row: Makai Mann ('16), Ellen Kaushansky ('16), Corban Swain ('16). Top row: Eddie King III ('15), Dylan Simonsen ('14), Michele Hall ('14).

Habit Lesson 7: Seek meaning and purpose.

Figure out your passion, be able to talk about it and talk about it all the time. It will be something that you know better than anyone else. It may take time for this to become clear. As you discover your own particular strengths, talents and interests, you can begin to focus time on clarifying your purpose. Then you can make this a habit. Find ways to live out your purpose in meaningful ways.

Dear Dean McLeod,

I've been in NYC working for Merrill Lynch since graduation and things at work have been going quite well. I received a promotion at the beginning of the year and have become a very integral part of my team.

However, just a few months in, I realized that this job wasn't my passion. That was when I decided to start thehungryhutch.com blog as a means to nurture what I feel compelled to do with my life in sharing my love of food with the world. Although I love the taste of a good dish in and of itself, what I truly enjoy is the meal — the time spent sharing stories, advice, jokes and an all-in-all good time with family, friends or even strangers. As a result, I'll be attending the French Culinary Institute part time starting in just two weeks.

Love,

Aaron

Aaron Hutcherson, Class of 2009
Major: Finance and Systems Science and Engineering
Currently a line cook at Northern Spy Food Co. in New York City and a freelance food stylist and writer

I have cherished the ideal of a democratic and free society in which all persons live together in harmony and with equal opportunities. It is an ideal which I hope to live for and to achieve. But if needs be, it is an ideal for which I am prepared to die.

— Nelson Mandela, April 20, 1964, Rivonia Trial

"Being an Ervin Scholar and knowing Dean McLeod has been a tremendous joy for me and has opened up many, many, many doors. Jim McLeod really encouraged me to follow my passions and think outside the box and be true to myself and my career and what I wanted to do in my service to people. Through Dean McLeod's motivation, I applied and got into Stanford for my PhD, completed that in molecular pharmacology, then went on to do a post-doc in oncology research. Now I'm a scientist at a biotech company."

Christopher Murriel, Class of 1998
Major: Chemistry
Currently a cancer research scientist with the biotechnology company OncoMed Pharmaceuticals

"Dean McLeod changed my life. Plain and simple. From the age of six, I knew I wanted to make movies, but it wasn't until my senior year in college that I had the chance to do so, and it was because of Dean McLeod. We sat down in his office before my senior year, and he agreed immediately — both financially and administratively — to support the production of the first-ever feature-length movie shot at Washington University, based on a screenplay that I wrote.

The project became my Honors thesis, and it absolutely consumed my life and the life of my producing partner, Natalie Kiwi. Entitled 'Four Years,' the project premiered on campus to three sold-out shows. Close to 1,000 students came to see it, while others were turned away. Because of the enormous outpouring of support, for the first time ever, Washington University began to offer a film minor [now the Film and Media Studies Program in Arts & Sciences] and began to hire full-time faculty to teach film. …

Since leaving Washington University, I've managed to follow my dream — the dream he helped make possible — and have become a professional screenwriter."

Barry L. Levy, Class of 1994
Major: Psychology
Currently a screenwriter in California; his credits include *Vantage Point* and *Paranoia*

JAMES EARL MCLEOD: A LIFE WELL-LIVED

When people speak about the late James E. "Jim" McLeod, they call him "humble," "caring," "warm," "humane," "a good listener," "a moral compass" and "a genius." They knew him as mentor, colleague, teacher, husband, father, trusted adviser and friend. Many Washington University students whose lives he touched — and often changed — during his 37-year career at the university have said, "I hope that I can grow up to be more like him."

"If he had flaws (other than a messy office), I never saw them," says Ervin Scholar Gregg Walker (Class of 1994).

Herb Weitman

Gregg Walker and his parents pose at his Commencement ceremony in 1994.

Through a chorus of voices — through the funny, sad, wry, poignant stories people tell about him — a portrait emerges of a man who had a remarkable impact on others. It is clear that he cared deeply for Washington University in St. Louis and for each and every student with whom he came in contact. He wanted to know who they were, what they were interested in, how they were faring academically, what kind of family and community sustained them. Ultimately, he said, he wanted each student to be known "by name and by story."

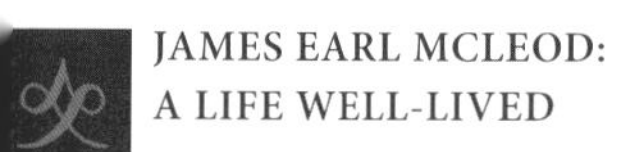

By Name and By Story

His own name: "To his family and closest friends, he was Sonny; to his wife, Clara, he was James," begins a tribute to McLeod in the February 2012 *Washington Magazine*. "Around the university, where he spent his 37-year career, admiring colleagues called him Jim, while his longtime assistant director in the Ervin Scholars Program, Dorothy Elliott, dubbed him 'the Chief.' …

James E. McLeod

James McLeod's family in 1959: (left to right) Alice, Mrs. H. Earline, Jeff, Rev. James C. and Mary McLeod at the Hartford Church of God in Christ, Hartford, Ala.

"But to thousands of students, he was — and always will be — Dean McLeod. Officially, that was his title." In 1992, he was named dean of the College of Arts & Sciences — one of a series of increasingly challenging administrative positions he held during his time at Washington University.

His own story: James Earl McLeod was born in Dothan, Ala., on July 29, 1944, the first son of Rev. James C. McLeod and H. Earline McLeod. Eventually, the household included two younger brothers, Jacob (who passed away as an infant) and Jeff, and sisters Alice and Mary.

It was a close-knit family during a difficult time in our nation's history when segregation was a fact of everyday life. Washington University was not immune

JAMES EARL MCLEOD'S LIFE AT-A-GLANCE

1944

Born July 29 in Dothan, Ala., the first son of Rev. James C. McLeod and H. Earline McLeod

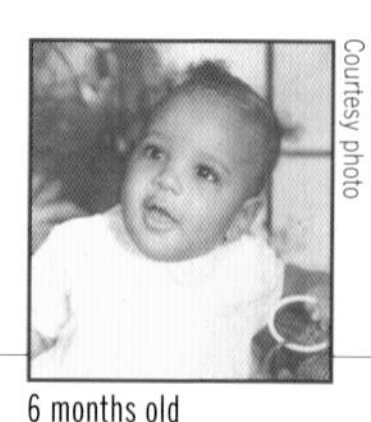

Courtesy photo

6 months old

Courtesy photo

7 years old, 1951

His brother Jeff says "Sonny" often heard the "mantra that my father preached and modeled: 'Bite off more than you can chew, and chew it anyway.'"

from that history; its undergraduate programs finally opened to African Americans on May 9, 1952, under a somewhat-reluctant Chancellor Arthur Holly Compton, when James McLeod was eight years old. Decades later, as the dean and vice chancellor for students, he would become a leader of those same undergraduate programs.

Courtesy photo

Sister Mary and James

McLeod always spoke warmly about his family. From his grandfather and father, he learned about farming, the benefits of focus and hard work and developed a love for God's gift of land and trees.

He once said, "I would not have made it but for the few lessons my parents chose to teach me. Only a few things mattered to them: the difference between right and wrong – the ability to read and write – the nobility of work – the necessity for homework before play – and most importantly, it's not just about you.

Courtesy photo

James McLeod (right) and his brother Jeff

1960

Entered Morehouse College at age 16

The Torch

Freshman year

1963–65

Studied with the Institute of European Studies at the University of Vienna

Dothan Eagle

SUNDAY, SEPTEMBER 1, 1963

Negro Student Goes To Europe

A Dothan Negro, James E. McLeod, a junior at Morehouse College, Atlanta, is one of 154 students en route to Europe to begin a year's study at the University of Vienna. He is the son of James C. McLeod, 738 Tuskegee St.

"I would not have made it without sisters and a brother who could throw punches as well as hugs. No matter how mad you got, you had to share the same dinner table and share the same bed."

His brother Jeff says "Sonny" often heard the "mantra that my father preached and modeled: 'Bite off more than you can chew, and chew it anyway.'"

From his family, he also learned the value of faith, which was a significant part of his life, as was the power of education. In 2001, he told a *Washington Magazine* interviewer that education, "was this thing you must get. Although most of my classmates didn't go to college, there was never any debate about it in my family. My parents managed to send all four of us — of course, we worked, borrowed and got scholarships, too — but it was a great sacrifice to them."

The Torch

James McLeod (third from right) in 1963 joins other Morehouse College students who had been awarded Merrill Travel scholarships to spend their junior year abroad.

In large part his background helped McLeod become what Jerome Strickland (Ervin Scholar 2002) called an "ever-present moral and intellectual compass" for Washington University undergraduates.

His family's emphasis on education as a passport to a better life led James McLeod

1966

Received a bachelor's degree from Morehouse College in German and chemistry

1966–71

Graduate studies in German at Rice University, where he was a National Defense Education Act Fellow and Woodrow Wilson Fellow

1967

Married Clara Prioleau

Courtesy photo

Clara Prioleau

to enroll at Morehouse College in Atlanta in 1960 at age 16. The civil rights movement had begun and Martin Luther King, Jr., himself a Morehouse alumnus and co-pastor of Ebenezer Baptist Church, gave regular talks on campus. "It was a very heady time and place," McLeod said. He also met and fell in love with Clara Prioleau, who was studying biology at Spelman College.

Courtesy photo

James McLeod (right) Priscilla Camp and Clara McLeod (left) work in the garden in July 1976.

Courtesy photo

McLeod with fellow students of the Institute for European Studies studying at the University of Vienna

At Morehouse, he encountered the concept of the "Morehouse Man" — a Renaissance man with a social conscience, a citizen of the world, acquainted with languages and cultures. He said that Morehouse also "showed me that, if a student steps out and participates, he will learn better. College is not a spectator sport. If you sit back and simply observe, you are not going to get a good education."

A legendary Morehouse chemistry professor, Henry C. McBay, inspired McLeod to major in chemistry. But he also spent the first summer of his freshman year participating in Operation Crossroads Africa; later he studied at the Institute of European Studies at the University of Vienna. There he became passionately interested in Austrian literature and the German language, which were to become his academic focus.

1971–74

Faculty member at Indiana University in Bloomington

1974

Came to Washington University in St. Louis as assistant professor of German and assistant dean of the Graduate School of Arts & Sciences

James E. McLeod

Professor James F. Poag and his wife Juliane

WU Office of Information

Ralph E. Morrow

He graduated from Morehouse in 1966 with a bachelor's degree in chemistry and German, then began graduate studies in German at Rice University in Houston, where he was a National Defense Education Act Fellow and Woodrow Wilson Fellow. His research included the cultural history of turn-of-the-century Vienna and post-war Germany. During graduate school he developed a lifelong love for photography.

Courtesy photo

James McLeod married Clara Prioleau in 1967.

He and Clara married in 1967. He left Rice University in 1971 to teach German at Indiana University in Bloomington and remained there until 1974.

A "Very Special Place"

While teaching at Indiana University, McLeod learned from a friend, James Poag, PhD, now Washington University professor emeritus of German, that a position was open at Washington University, so he applied and was hired. At age 30, McLeod came to the university in 1974 as assistant professor of German, in the Department of Germanic Languages & Literatures, and as assistant dean of the Graduate School of Arts & Sciences. At the time, Ralph E. Morrow was dean of the Graduate School and became a mentor to his younger colleague.

WUSTL Photos

1977–87

Assistant to Chancellor William H. Danforth

Herb Weitman

William and Elizabeth "Ibby" Danforth

1986

Welcomed daughter Sara Elizabeth

James E. McLeod

Sara McLeod

In St. Louis, he gained a community and an academic home. He said, "Here I found a place where a guy from Alabama, shaped by Carver High School, Morehouse College and Rice University could be accepted, included and invited to participate in a grand and glorious vision to be a very special place for young people to come of age and prepare themselves for life by getting a great education."

Courtesy photo

James McLeod's Carver High School photo, 1957–58

Among those who welcomed the young German professor to the university was John B. Ervin, PhD, at that time dean of the School of Continuing Education (now University College). When McLeod met Ervin, he introduced himself and Ervin said, "Welcome. I've been expecting you."

From his family, he also learned the value of faith, which was a significant part of his life, as was the power of education.

McLeod's colleague in the German department, Egon Schwarz, PhD, the Rosa May Distinguished Professor Emeritus in the Humanities, remembers that McLeod's "love of German" began during his time at Morehouse College.

Schwarz says, "I use the word 'German' here as a linguistic term because Jim's primary interest and expertise were in things Austrian." While spending time at the University of Vienna, McLeod "was so

1987–92

Director of the African and Afro-American Studies Program in Arts & Sciences

Washington University Archives

McLeod teaching German

1987–2011

Director of the John B. Ervin Scholars Program

Warren Pottinger ('93)

enthralled by the city's vibrant culture that he persuaded the reluctant Morehouse president to send him back for a second year. The intellectual impregnation he received enabled him to make this his field of learning for his PhD studies and later teach very broadly conceived courses to enthusiastic students in the German department at Washington University."

Three years after McLeod's arrival, William H. Danforth, MD, the university's 13th chancellor, 1971–95 (and now Chancellor Emeritus), tapped Professor McLeod to be his assistant, a post McLeod held from 1977–87. A highlight of his personal life during those years came in 1986 when he and Clara welcomed their daughter Sara Elizabeth to the family. He loved to tell stories about Sara to underscore a salient point about how she tried his patience, but he also said, "She remains the love of our lives."

Washington University Archives

Professor McLeod taught German to "enthusiastic students," says Egon Schwarz, his colleague from the German department. In 1991, McLeod was awarded Washington University's Distinguished Faculty Award.

In his working life, McLeod was inspired by Danforth's "very deep commitment" to the university. Years later he told an interviewer, "I grew up in Alabama in the '50s and '60s. This idea of how one can *trust* an organization was big for me."

To illustrate the character of his relationship with McLeod, Danforth remembers one time when McLeod proved his mettle. "Courage was an essential part of Jim,"

1991	1992–2011	1995–2011	1997
Received Washington University's Distinguished Faculty Award	Dean of the College of Arts & Sciences	Also Vice Chancellor for Students	Master of ceremonies at the retirement event for Gloria White, vice chancellor for human resources

Courtesy photo

McLeod with his young daughter, Sara Elizabeth

he says. "He was always calm, quiet, gentle, never bending to the fashion of the day or to the passions of an unruly crowd.

"Some years ago I was invited to attend a meeting organized by a black faculty member to hear criticisms of Washington University and its chancellor. This was not the first such meeting. Students referred to [it as] 'maomaoing the chancellor.' I went to a room in Mallinckrodt Center. There was a table in front with two chairs. The convening faculty member sat in one; so I sat in the other.

"Before we started I heard a noise and found that Jim McLeod had pulled up a chair and was sitting next to me. As we walked away from the meeting, I said, 'Jim, I just hope that if a bunch of white guys ever get after you, I'll have the courage to sit next to you.' Jim was kind to those of us with crazy ideas but, when principle was at stake, he never gave an inch."

Recognizing the steadiness and wisdom of his assistant, Chancellor Danforth asked McLeod in 1986 to consider ways to improve the recruitment of African-American undergraduate students to Washington University. Minority enrollment had reached a low in the mid-1980s, and the number of minority

Joe Angeles

McLeod with Gloria White

Courtesy photo

McLeod with his father in 2001

2007

Awarded Rosa L. Parks Award for Meritorious Service to the Community (with William H. Danforth)

2007

Named one of St. Louis' Most Influential Minority Business Leaders by the *St. Louis Business Journal*

students — especially African-American students — in that fall's freshman class was disappointing.

Working with Stephanie Lewis, president of the Association of Black Students, McLeod suggested the Ervin Scholars Program as a way to draw African-American students to the university and became the program's champion. More than just a scholarship program, it would bring Ervin Scholars together as a community. The program was to be open to students from the United States entering any of the university's undergraduate divisions: Architecture, Art, Arts & Sciences, Business and Engineering.

Courtesy Ervin Scholars Program

Carla Cartwright, Christopher Brummer, Joy Coleman and Lisa Bourne — all Ervin Scholars from the Class of 1997 — were named to Phi Beta Kappa in spring 1997.

Initially called the "John B. Ervin Scholars Program for Black Americans," the program was named to honor Dr. John B. Ervin, colleague and friend to Chancellor Danforth and McLeod and a well-respected black educator. Ervin, the first African American named a dean at Washington University, served as dean of Continuing Education from 1968–77, then as a vice president at the Danforth Foundation.

The undergraduate admissions office, McLeod and others spent the 1986–87 academic year recruiting the first class of Ervin Scholars. In fall 1987, 11 students arrived to initiate the program.

2008

Received Salute to Excellence in Education Lifetime Achievement Award from *St. Louis American*

2010

Received Washington University's "Search" Award from the William Greenleaf Eliot Society: (right) Chancellor Mark Wrighton, McLeod, Chancellor Emeritus William Danforth

Joe Angeles

2010 Search Award

A Program Takes Shape

In 1987, Jim McLeod was named director of the Ervin Scholars Program as well as director of the African and Afro-American Studies Program (now African and African-American Studies) in Arts & Sciences.

As director, McLeod made Dr. Ervin's principles and values the touchstones of the program. He enumerated those to an interviewer in 2011:

- academic, intellectual achievement and engagement
- education's redemptive qualities, making a difference in the life of an individual and in the life of a community
- providing service to the community as an act of leadership
- engagement with some activity or purpose in a substantive way
- diversity, healing deep divisions within a community by finding ways to work with individuals and groups very different from you.

JOHN B. ERVIN SCHOLARS PROGRAM, THE FIRST 25 YEARS

1986

Announcement of the new Ervin Scholars Program for Black Americans appears in the Washington University *Record*. Concerned about the low number of undergraduate minority students entering the university in 1986, Chancellor William H. Danforth asks his special assistant, James E. McLeod, "to think about how we could approach" the issue of minority recruiting. Thus was born the idea for the Ervin Scholars Program.

Herb Weitman

Dr. John B. Ervin

1986–87

Recruiting takes place for the first class of Ervin Scholars who will enter the university in fall 1987.

1987

The first class of 11 Ervin Scholars arrives with James E. McLeod as the program's director.

2010

McLeod Scholars Program at Washington University established in his honor

Mary Butkus

McLeod Scholars Program reception, May 2010

2010

The first class of McLeod Scholars entered Washington University

2011

Received Coro Leadership Award

2011

Died September 6

Highlights of James E. McLeod's Community Service

Board chair, Express Scripts Foundation

Board member, American Youth Foundation

Board member, Churchill Center & School for Learning Disabilities

Board member, Mary Institute Country Day School

Board member, National Council on Youth Leadership

Board member, Saint Louis Art Museum

Board member, The Civil Rights Project, Inc.

Board of directors, Christian Hospital Northeast Northwest, 1994–2004

Chair of board, board member, chair of advisory council, New City School

Founding board member, Forest Park Forever; director 1986–94

President, St. Louis Chapter of the Morehouse Alumni Society, 1976–79 Vice President of Midwest Region, 1982

University representative to Skinker DeBaliviere Community Council

Joe Angeles

The McLeod family when Dean McLeod received the Eliot Society "Search" Award in 2010: (standing): Clara, James E., and Sara McLeod (seated): Rev. James C. McLeod

McLeod commented, "We don't [often] talk that way any more. So I think it's doubly important to re-emphasize that John Ervin came at a time when education for persons of his background just wasn't assumed as something easy and available to get. Today things that he struggled for are taken for granted."

While McLeod, with typical humility, gave credit to John Ervin and deflected attention from himself, he was the one who became the face and voice of the program, the students' mentor, teacher, father figure and role model.

Eboni Sharp (Ervin Scholar 2014) says, "He played such a large role in the way I view myself as a student, but most of all as a person. For Ervin Scholars, he was our 'Daddy' McLeod, our father away from home who cared deeply for each of us and always sought to help ensure our personal success.

"He always saw a light in me, a sort of sparkle that set me apart and made me special, even when I didn't see it myself. I hope to be half the person he was someday."

His warmth and genuine caring about each individual helped students to adapt and to succeed at the university, but so did the high standards and expectations he set. Charles Brown, Jr. (Ervin Scholar 1996) told the *St. Louis American* in September 2011, "He had the

On September 15, 2003, four Washington University graduates and Rhodes Scholars returned to campus to share their experiences with current students and to participate in an interactive panel discussion: (left to right) Sarah Johnson ('01); Ervin Scholar Trina (Williams) Shanks ('92); Ben Cannon ('99); and Ian Klaus ('01).

1986

Dorothy Elliott (below right, with McLeod) becomes assistant director of the program.

1987

Adrienne Glore (above left), from the dean of students office, joins the program staff.

1991

The first class of Ervin Scholars graduates.

1992

John B. Ervin passes away on October 7. He had the opportunity to meet the first four classes of Ervin Scholars.

1993

The dedication of the John B. Ervin memorial bench (below) takes place on Brookings Quadrangle. After that, the bench commemoration becomes an annual fall event.

expectation for all students — not just the scholars — to develop a responsibility ... towards self and towards the global community. He wanted the scholars to embrace community leadership as much as he expected us to embrace academic excellence."

Gregg Walker (Ervin Scholar 1994) comments, "Dean McLeod saw all my flaws, yet he never judged me. He set the highest standards; he exemplified excellence, and he demanded excellence."

Students and colleagues recall how McLeod would greet them on campus and listen to them with undivided attention. "He was vice chancellor for students, and he would stop and talk to you no matter what he was doing," Kelley Greenman (Ervin Scholar 2009) says. "It didn't matter if he was on his way to a board of trustees meeting or hanging out in the Danforth University Center. I would get the warmest hug from him." He would ask about what was going on in her life and whether she was achieving the expectations she set for herself.

Courtesy Photo

Shaun Koiner ('04), while working as an undergraduate admissions officer at Washington University, joined the admissions receptionist, Delise Le Pool, at an admissions presentation.

Students even recall the way he listened. At the dedication of McLeod's Way on September 15, 2012, Shaun Koiner (Ervin Scholar 2004) remembered many of Dean McLeod's endearing quirks, saying, "What made the Dean McLeod

Jerry Naunheim

McLeod's Way was dedicated on September 15, 2012, in James McLeod's memory. (left to right) Chancellor Emeritus William H. Danforth; McLeod's daughter Sara, wife Clara, nephew Jeffrey, brother Jeff; Risa Zwerling Wrighton, Chancellor Mark S. Wrighton

connection ... was how he greeted you: wide smile, hug or bro-hug, hands behind the back, and he would rock and sometimes that left leg would lift when you hit him with something particularly appealing."

Yet, being the center of Jim McLeod's attention and having him know so much about your life was not always comfortable. "A lot of people talk about the hugs and the touches, but he knew when you needed a hard word, when you needed a strong hand, when you needed to be pushed and challenged to dig deeper inside of yourself," Ed Stowe (Ervin Scholar 1998) says. While he was a student, Stowe had decided to leave the university and thought he was just going to pack up and go.

1998

The Ervin Scholars Program receives $3 million in endowment — part of a $100 million Danforth Foundation gift to the *Campaign for Washington University.*

1998

Tenth anniversary celebration takes place in the spring.

1999

The first winter retreat takes place in January.

1999

The first Ervin Exploration Weekend is held in the fall (now part of Fall Discovery Weekend).

2000

Monica C. Lewis (below), Ervin Scholar Class of 1999, writes "A Legacy of Excellence: A History of the John B. Ervin Scholars Program at Washington University in St. Louis," the first installment in a history of the program.

Courtesy Photo

"James E. McLeod had learned through some friends of mine of my impending decision," Stowe says. "He got ahold of me and we talked. This was not one of those warm, fuzzy, supportive, you-can-do-anything-you-dream-of kind of talks. It was one of those talks you get from your dad. It was a talk of some very hard words that I had to hear. And embrace.

"I can honestly say, that was one of the milestones of my life here. He challenged me very quickly to finish what I started, whether here or anywhere else. He knew a lot of the background of why I chose Washington University — because of the challenge it would present — and he reminded me of that.

"I automatically bemoaned the fact that it would take at least an extra semester. He looked at me and said, 'Well that's probably because it's not time for you to leave yet.'"

McLeod taught these life lessons through his words and deeds; beginning in 1991, he also shared some guidelines with new scholars at the Ervin orientation. Each

Sid Hastings

This bench in Brookings Quadrangle, dedicated on September 16, 2012 in memory of Dean McLeod, was a gift from the Black Alumni Council and friends of the university.

Sid Hastings

Mrs. Jane Ervin and her grandson Marcus Creighton were participants in the Ervin Scholars Program 25th anniversary celebration in September 2012. Here they attend the McLeod's Way dedication ceremony in Graham Chapel.

August, he gave his Habits of Achievement talk, sometimes swapping out the personal anecdotes he used to illustrate how the "habits" might play out in students' lives.

"Dean McLeod made all of us students feel as though we were the most important people on the planet," Jerome Strickland (Ervin Scholar 2002) told *St. Louis American* in September 2011. "His 'Habits of Achievement' lessons ingrained in me and my peers a more intense commitment to disciplined preparation in all areas of our lives."

2001

Washington University announces a $25 million gift (below) on October 18, 2001, to establish the Enterprise Rent-A-Car Scholarships; a portion of them are designated for students chosen through the Ervin Scholars Program. (Today, the program is called Enterprise Holdings Scholarships.)

Joe Angeles

(left to right) John F. McDonnell, chairman, WUSTL board of trustees; Andrew C. Taylor, Enterprise Rent-A-Car chairman and CEO; Chancellor Mark S. Wrighton, James E. McLeod

2002

Fifteenth anniversary celebration takes place.

2002

Mrs. Dorothy Elliott, assistant director of the Ervin Program, retires. She remains engaged with the scholars as alumni director.

2003

Laura Stephenson becomes assistant director of the program.

Not only did the Ervin Scholars Program have high expectations, it also developed cherished traditions. Students gather together several times a year for special events — to commemorate the John B. Ervin Bench in Brookings Quadrangle, to celebrate the birthday of Mrs. Jane Ervin, and for orientation and a winter retreat, including the newly named McLeod Day of Service. (Today a bench dedicated to the memory of James E. McLeod also sits in Brookings Quadrangle, a gift from the Black Alumni Council and friends of the university.) Once Ervin Scholars had graduated and made their way into the world, there were program accomplishments to sustain the Ervin community and to pass on to new scholars.

Sid Hastings

A group photo of Ervin Scholars who attended the 25th anniversary celebration, September 15, 2012.

Other scholarships established at the university, such as the Annika Rodriguez Scholars and the Danforth Scholars programs, drew on the success of the Ervin Scholars to develop their own directions and traditions.

In 2004, Washington University reconsidered the criteria for admission to the Ervin Program as the result of two University of Michigan legal cases, deliberated in spring 2003, that involved the use of race in undergraduate and law school admissions. While one Supreme Court ruling appeared to support race as a viable factor in admissions policies, the national discussion suggested that continuing to keep the Ervin Scholars Program open only to African-American students could cause the university to lose federal funding.

Sid Hastings

Gerald Early, the Merle Kling Professor of Modern Letters, remembers James McLeod as an effective leader of the African and Afro-American Studies Program.

As director, McLeod led the transition to opening the Ervin Scholars Program to all students who were U.S. citizens, while continuing to focus on academic achievement, community service, leadership, diversity, engagement and character.

He had an impact, too, in his role at the helm of the African and Afro-American Studies Program. Gerald Early, PhD, one of McLeod's colleagues in the program and now the Merle Kling Professor of Modern Letters, saw how McLeod interacted with the program's students, staff and faculty from his seemingly disorganized office:

2004

In April, Washington University announces that it will revise the criteria to select scholarship recipients for its Ervin Scholars Program. The program continues to foster a richly diverse educational atmosphere. It is now open to all U.S. students who are dedicated to academic excellence, community service, especially communities in need, leadership and diversity.

2007

Twentieth anniversary celebration: "Living the Legacy"

2007

A copy of the booklet *Legacies: A History of the John B. Ervin Scholars Program at Washington University in St. Louis* is given to those attending the 20th anniversary celebration. It combines a second installment of a history of the Ervin program — "A Legacy of Commitment," written by Michelle A. Purdy, Ervin Scholar Class of 2009 — with the first part written by Monica Lewis in 2000.

2010

Laura Stephenson leaves the program.

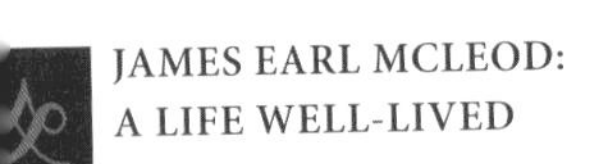

"I was a bit horrified when I entered his office. It seemed completely chaotic. His desk groaned with papers and files that seemed all helter-skelter. I could not imagine how he could ever find anything. As we talked, he took notes on small cards, and I was afraid that he would never look at those cards again. He had a lot of them. … In fact, I was afraid my request was going to disappear somewhere in the disorder, the utter black hole, of his office and not be found until after I retired.

"He approved my request, but I left his office convinced that I would never see the fruit of it. … I expected any day to hear about the complete collapse of African and African-American Studies, ground to a halt as the director was reported buried under an avalanche of his own debris.

"In a few days, though, I received what I had asked for. I received everything I wanted from Jim — just what I wanted when I wanted it. He never forgot a request, a favor, a question or a suggestion. Everything always seemed on the brink of utter breakdown with Jim's seeming disorganization, yet under Jim things in Afro-Am ran amazingly well, much better than they ever had before.

Joe Angeles

James McLeod, Trustee Andrew M. Bursky and Clara McLeod (foreground) listen to remarks at the McLeod Scholars Program reception on May 6, 2010.

"Jim, in his quiet way, inspired people: The students were very fond of him because he listened to them and the staff quite dedicated to him, although I think he expected a lot from them. But he seemed to make them feel that they ought to give it. In fact, that is probably why they were so dedicated to him; he thought they could do far more than they had done before — and so did they."

Dean McLeod

The university recognized the impact of Jim McLeod's work by awarding him a Distinguished Faculty Award at Founders Day 1991.

In 1992 McLeod broadened the scope of his work with students and faculty when he became dean of the College of Arts & Sciences while remaining director of the Ervin Scholars Program. "Jim was a remarkably kind teacher, colleague and boss. His voice was soft and gentle. He was everyone's friend and supporter," William H. Danforth said. "Yet he never expected us to slack off, but to give our best and then, when we had, to aim higher. He gave gentle suggestions. Then if we didn't get it the first, second or fifth time, he just kept reminding us of what was right and wise until we saw the light, and realized, 'Jim was right all along.'"

Regina Frey, PhD, the Florence E. Moog Professor of STEM Education and executive director of the Teaching Center, concurs. She said, "Jim was a wonderful mentor. He gave me sage advice over the years about teaching and specifically teaching *General Chemistry*. As with all students, I did not always follow his advice immediately. And I regretted it every time I did not. However, Jim was very patient with me."

2010

Margaret West (below) becomes associate director of the program and assistant dean of the College of Arts & Sciences.

David Kilper

2010

The first class of McLeod Scholars — three students — arrives to begin their freshman year. One of them, Michele Hall, is also selected as an Ervin Scholar.

Mary Butkus

The first-ever cohort of James E. McLeod Scholars — Ana Solorio, Michele Hall and Dylan Simonsen, Class of 2014

2011

James E. McLeod, director of the Ervin Scholars Program since its inception, passes away on September 6.

James E. McLeod

The former, longtime Parkmoor restaurant in St. Louis was a perfect setting for breakfast meetings of Ed Macias and Jim McLeod for 20 years.

Because of McLeod's warmth, quick smile and ready hugs, many faculty members felt as Provost Edward S. Macias, PhD, did: "Jim McLeod was … one of my closest friends." Macias continues, "But the amazing thing about Jim is that so many people feel he was a close friend. …

"We met for breakfast every other week for 20 years. In the beginning … we met at the Parkmoor restaurant. That was the best place for us: its décor was vintage Naugahyde; the waitresses left us alone — to the point of ignoring us. That was important because we normally met for two and one-half hours, beginning at 7:30 in the morning. And most importantly, they had grits. Good grits are the key to a good breakfast."

What made McLeod so effective in his role as dean was that he always kept students in the forefront, creating a student-centered place that allowed them to thrive. He wanted them to have an extraordinary experience both inside and outside the classroom.

"Many of the great advances of Washington University have been conceived and shepherded by Jim McLeod," said William H. Danforth. "Chief among these is the development of a marvelous undergraduate culture involving faculty, staff and students all working together to provide an atmosphere that encourages and supports growth in learning, in the ability to work with and understand others, in leadership skills, in responsible behavior and in making progress on clarifying and working toward one's highest aspirations."

When McLeod added the role of vice chancellor for students to his role as dean in 1995, he added campus life and students' on-campus residential experiences to his portfolio. Richard A. Roloff, then vice chancellor for capital projects, recalls, "Jim was concerned about the students having accommodations that were something they would feel at home in. He had a vision of what was needed. The new student housing and the Danforth University Center are examples of his dreams."

Among the changes McLeod brought to the undergraduate experience were a residential college approach to dormitory living, a strengthened undergraduate advising system, new small-group

Kevin Lowder

Leading the way: Dean McLeod walks the lead lap at the 2011 Relay For Life fundraiser for the American Cancer Society with cancer survivors (left to right) students Kyle Newton, Briana Keightley, Jordan Wagner, Annie Wallentine, Eric Teng and McLeod. Ervin Scholar Sacha Coupet ('91) says that McLeod taught her "many things about being confident and brave in the face of fear."

2012

Twenty-fifth anniversary celebration, September 14–16: "25 Years of Achievement: Our Names and Our Stories"

Nyla (Batts) Smith ('05)

2012

Jerry Naunheim

Sara and Clara McLeod with Chancellor Wrighton at the McLeod's Way dedication

September 15: The dedication of McLeod's Way, a new landscaped gathering place on the South 40

Sid Hastings

Ervin Scholar Ron Herd ('02), Clara McLeod, Jane Ervin with Herd's painting of James McLeod and John Ervin

September 16: Dedication of the new Black Alumni Council bench, in Dean McLeod's memory, Brookings Quadrangle

"Jim touched the lives of thousands of students. He inspired them to achieve more than they imagined."

—Mark S. Wrighton, Chancellor

housing, a new undergraduate curriculum in Arts & Sciences, a richer mix of seminar experiences for freshmen, and helping to initiate and shape an expanded year-abroad program.

"Jim touched the lives of thousands of students," said Chancellor Mark S. Wrighton, PhD. "He inspired them to achieve more than they imagined and he developed and mobilized a great team of professionals to work with them.

"He was my most trusted adviser on all matters affecting the lives of undergraduate students."

Illustration by Steve Edwards, BFA 1987

Members of the Washington University community celebrate Jim McLeod's 25 years at Washington University in 1999.

McLeod's respect for students came across in his expectations for them and in the way he treated them.

One graduate student recalls a "wonderful talk" that McLeod gave to graduate students each year at the university's Teaching Assistant orientation. Many new TAs believed it was the most useful, memorable part of the event, since he helped them understand and appreciate the undergraduates they would be teaching:

Sid Hastings

Ervin Scholars Program leaders gather at the 25th anniversary gala celebration: (left to right) Laura Stephenson, Dorothy Elliott, Adrienne Glore, Wilmetta Toliver-Diallo and Margaret West. The John B. Ervin drawing behind them is the work of Ervin Scholar Warren Pottinger, Class of 1993.

"Treat them as adults, even when they don't seem to deserve it."

"'When you see a student who needs help, please tell us' in the College office."

Students who were struggling — with an academic subject, a serious illness, the illness or death of a parent, a change in financial circumstances or some difficulty adjusting to college life — often turned to him for advice. He always pointed them toward a solution or to someone else at the university who could help them. Many credit him with making it possible to stay in school and to graduate.

If a student was in trouble, however, and didn't tell him the truth, he used that as a teachable moment. Ervin Scholar Kim Daily (Class of 2011) remembers, "I lied to Dean McLeod once. Yeah, it was bad." After an Ervin class meeting around midterms he asked her how she was doing in school.

> **"We all acknowledge the great mystery of our presence on this planet. I acknowledge how fortunate I am and I cannot account for my good fortune by tallying the few things I do each day. So, I can say I have been bountifully blessed and I am humbled by the bounty of that blessing."**
>
> — James E. McLeod, 2008 Remarks upon receiving *St. Louis American's* Salute to Excellence in Education Lifetime Achievement Award

Jerry Naunheim

Clara and James McLeod stop and speak with a student on campus. Students recall "he would stop and talk to you no matter what he was doing."

"I was like, 'I'm great, Dean McLeod.'

"'How's chemistry?'

"'It's going well; it's going super.'

"I had a D in the class. He knew that. So I got an email, I'm pretty sure a couple hours later, saying 'Make an appointment with me and Laura (Stephenson), and we will talk about how well you're doing in chemistry.'

"So that was one of the biggest mistakes of my life, trying to lie to Dean McLeod, as if he didn't know I wasn't succeeding in *General Chemistry.*"

Toward the end of the semester Dean McLeod suggested that Kim Daily and Brianna Davis (Ervin Scholar 2011) have a chemistry study party to help them with finals and that they ought to have pizza, which he would buy for them. "He was a man of his word, and we had a pizza paid for by Dean McLeod for us to succeed in life," Daily says.

He continued to focus on students even after he found himself facing a serious illness. In 2009 he was diagnosed with cancer and underwent treatment, but as soon as he was able, he resumed his demanding schedule.

Courtesy Photo

Marilyn Chill, director of operations in the College of Arts & Sciences, and Patti Randall, administrative aide, worked closely with James McLeod in his role as dean of the College. They show off the plaque for the conference room in Cupples II Hall named in McLeod's memory in 2012.

In 2010, Washington University honored him by establishing the James E. McLeod Scholars Program; he also received the "Search" award from the university's William Greenleaf Eliot Society. That year, he was able to spend time with the first class of McLeod Scholars, three students who entered the university in fall 2010.

When his illness returned, he maintained his work schedule as best he could. His wife Clara asked him if he had considered retiring, but he told her he was doing what he wanted to do. "He would say, 'I can't let my bosses know how much I enjoy my work,'" she recalls.

He greeted the members of the incoming class and their parents in August 2011. He died on September 6, 2011.

When asked how he wanted to be remembered, Dean McLeod frequently said "as a decent human being."

When asked how he wanted to be remembered, Dean McLeod frequently said "as a decent human being." The tributes and stories that have poured in since his untimely death show that he was that and so much more.

"When I come to Washington University, I see him everywhere," says Robert L. Virgil, MBA, DBA, emeritus trustee, dean and professor who received an honorary doctor of laws degree in 2009. "I see him in the students — their growth and development during their time here, the fun they have, their diversity, their inclusiveness, their community service, what they accomplish as alumni. In short, I see Jim in the culture of the campus and the undergraduate experience. This culture was his work. He was the architect."

Courtesy Photo

This bench on the South 40 residential area is inscribed with one of McLeod's favorite sayings: "Learning is not a spectator sport."

Courtesy Photo

Dean and Clara McLeod (left) attend a class meeting with Ervin Scholars from the Class of 2013.

AFTERWORD

Wayne Fields, PhD, has been a friend of the Ervin Scholars Program since its inception. He was a close friend of both the late John B. Ervin and the late James E. McLeod. He gave the following address at the Recognition Ceremony for the College of Arts & Sciences graduating class at Commencement in May 2012.

Congratulations to the Arts & Sciences graduates of 2012, and to your families and friends.

Joe Angeles

Wayne Fields

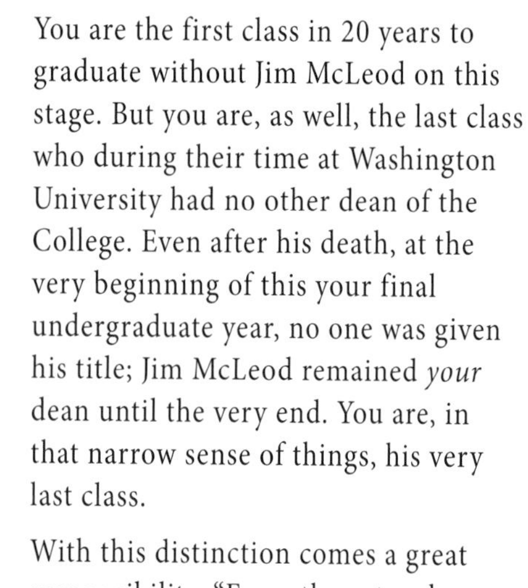

You are the first class in 20 years to graduate without Jim McLeod on this stage. But you are, as well, the last class who during their time at Washington University had no other dean of the College. Even after his death, at the very beginning of this your final undergraduate year, no one was given his title; Jim McLeod remained *your* dean until the very end. You are, in that narrow sense of things, his very last class.

With this distinction comes a great responsibility. "From those to whom much is given, much is required." You have been given much, given much by your families, by your teachers, by people you know well and people you will never meet, but part of that much which you've enjoyed, given to you out of his own personal grace and generosity, was Jim McLeod.

We began this school year in mourning, weighed down by the loss of a beloved mentor and friend. We now conclude in celebration both of your achievements and of the life that did so much to help you to realize more fully your gifts as students and as human beings. It is appropriate, then, for us to remember as you prepare to leave the college to which Dean McLeod gave so much of his life, what out of his own being he taught us, to remember it now with joy.

I have suggested that Jim was a gift to us, a gift in part of history. Remember that James Earl McLeod was born into an apartheid America, born at a time when efforts to dehumanize on the basis of skin color were everywhere visible. No opportunity for diminishment was too small, whether the issue was a drinking fountain or a public toilet; no person, no matter how young, was too innocent to brutalize. The year that Rosa Parks refused to give up her seat on a Montgomery, Ala., bus, Jim McLeod was an 11-year-old living in a town just a short bus ride away. When his state's governor, George Wallace, stood in the doorway to the University of Alabama in order to block the entrance of two African-American students, Jim McLeod was an undergraduate at Morehouse College in neighboring Georgia. And he was at Morehouse later that same year when a Ku Klux Klan bomber murdered four children attending Sunday school at the Sixteenth Street Baptist Church in Birmingham, only half a state removed from the church in which Jim's father was officiating.

This was an America terrifying in its deep fear of difference, and in its malignant obsession with race and power, a country in which, all too often, education was not just an exclusionary endeavor, it was a weapon in a vicious war against human dignity. This history stains our university as well. Jim was already eight years old when Washington University found the courage to end its own practice of segregation and institutional racism.

I am telling you these things from Jim's past fully aware that he never did — Jim focused on the present and the future, and he claimed no distinction either of accomplishment or grievance. But you should know something of the world in which he found his way, know so as not to take for granted the profound decency of the man, but also that you may better understand the education you have received under his stewardship.

Part of the reason Jim rarely spoke of the history through which he lived, was his knowledge that his was not an individual achievement — no significant achievement ever is. He was the product of a proud family, of a supportive congregation, of a vibrant African-American community, of great teachers. Morehouse is a great and distinguished college and Jim hardly suffered academically by being there rather than the smaller-minded university George Wallace would keep him from attending.

Like each of us, he was the product of many influences, owed much to many whose identities were unknown even to him much less to us. He was humbled by an awareness of those who had paid dearly for opportunities that came to him. He knew that we stand less on the shoulders of giants than on the willing backs of persons of more ordinary stature. So he told you little of this past, but you should know it, and with that knowing better understand the very foundations of what he has been teaching us all these years.

Having himself grown up in a strident age, Jim brought to us a remarkable sense of calm. Having seen an America that indulged a violent pettiness, he was himself remarkably at peace and never petty. Above all he was "considerate" in the most important sense of that much-abused word. By that I don't mean he was "nice" — that is too superficial for the meaningful interactions he thought we all deserve. Most of us are "nice," mostly because it is easy. Far harder is the serious regard that Jim brought to everyone he encountered, the earnest effort to learn our individual stories. This requires an attention to our faults and failings that "niceness" can avoid. It is a response that is critical as well as supportive, one that expects us to be our best even when we are satisfied to just get by. Such respect takes time, a thing in short supply for a dean charged with the well-being of an entire college. But Jim gave us time, learned who we are, what we might become. He took us seriously, not simply because he was a good person, but because such knowledge was essential to his vision of education.

The presumption with which southern governors blocked schoolhouse doors was based on two equally fallacious assertions: first that humanity is divisible into different *kinds*, subspecies essentially different from one another — a claim refuted by both our DNA and common sense; the second insisted on a fundamental sameness within these subgroups, a likeness that denied individuality — otherwise why would differences between groups matter so much? So they declared us different in *kind* yet homogeneous by *type*.

The seriousness Jim brought to each of us is half of an inversion he made to the assumptions I've just described. Jim's educational view rested on the conviction that each of us is unique, representing a confluence of talents and backgrounds and experiences never exactly duplicated in anyone else. On the other hand, in our human identity, we are essentially the same. We are *different* in type but *same* in kind.

Thus, Jim's deep commitment to the idea of a liberal arts education as an instrument of liberation, an education for free people intent on learning how to exercise that freedom responsibly, how to fulfill individual aspirations *and* serve a common good. Every thing he taught us depends on our capacity for intellectual and moral growth, growth that is only possible when we learn to see more fully, learn to see from multiple perspectives, learn to live in a world that is bigger than we are, learn *even to take leadership* in that world empowered by an education that allows us to contextualize without sacrificing principle. It is that largeness of vision that defines a *true* liberal arts education.

And Jim understood, above all, that a liberal arts college is a community even more than a curriculum, a community in which we learn from one another regardless of the job descriptions we carry. He grew up in a society terrified by difference, where the most insecure could deal with their weakness only by declaring their superiority. In contrast to the university whose homogeneity Gov. Wallace was trying to preserve, Jim embraced diversity, insisted by his individualized attention that we are all different, and taught us to take pride in what others fear. He taught this university — which a generation earlier would have rejected him as a student — not only how much we had wasted in those years of exclusion but how much we gained when we outgrew such a demeaning academic practice. He taught us that we *need one another,* that *all of us need all of us*. That we can only be whole together.

A university, despite the implications of that designation, is a much-divided entity: divided by disciplines, by generations, by all the distinctions and discriminations of the society in which it exists. Still Jim insisted we *would* be a community, and by dealing with our differences honestly, seriously, considerately, we would learn how much more was possible by mutual affiliation than by division into ghettoes of assumed likeness. His liberal education teaches us to think and live both largely and profoundly. It gives the courage to live with multiplicity and irony.

Jim McLeod believed with Dr. King that there is an arc in the moral universe that bends toward justice, and he also believed there is

— or at least should be — an arc in the growth of human beings, collectively and individually, towards a more complete vision of what it means to be human, a deeper commitment to the humane. The liberal education he encouraged in our College, the education you have now completed, has as its purpose an ambition to prepare us for more complete, more fulfilling lives.

The leadership Jim imagined for you is possible only if the liberal arts have helped you realize that you are part of something much more than yourself, and have given you the resources to face that largeness courageously. The purpose of education as Jim imagined it is neither celebrity nor wealth, but rather wholeness and decency. And so the doors George Wallace and other governors of Jim's youth tried so desperately to bar, he flung open. Their fear he replaced with hope, their anger with joy.

In August, a few days before you began your senior year, Jim McLeod welcomed a new class of entering students, just as four years before he welcomed you. His message was one of reassurance to anxious teenagers, the promise that this was a place of human beings rather than granite and ivy, the confidence that they could find themselves here, and the offering of a phone number in case any of them needed help.

There was no great summation of McLeod wisdom to make its way onto the best-seller lists and then turn to dust in the archives. Rather he chose *you*; the lives *you* lead to be the legacy *he* leaves. You are his last class. *You* are his last words.

Live accordingly. Live well. Live well.

—*Wayne Fields, the Lynne Cooper Harvey Distinguished Professor of English*

When Dean McLeod introduced new Ervin Scholars to the Habits of Achievement, he emphasized the importance of planning and budgeting time. He said that some of the tools required to do this were a watch and a calendar.

APPENDIX A: PLANNING TOOLS

Washington University in St. Louis

John B. Ervin Scholars Program

SEMESTER GOALS

Name ____________________

Date ____________________

PROFESSIONAL

- [ ] ____________________
- [ ] ____________________
- [ ] ____________________
- [ ] ____________________
- [ ] ____________________
- [ ] ____________________
- [ ] ____________________
- [ ] ____________________

Academic

- [ ] ____________________
- [ ] ____________________
- [ ] ____________________
- [ ] ____________________
- [ ] ____________________
- [ ] ____________________
- [ ] ____________________
- [ ] ____________________

Personal

- [ ] ____________________
- [ ] ____________________
- [ ] ____________________
- [ ] ____________________
- [ ] ____________________

SOCIAL

- [ ] ____________________
- [ ] ____________________
- [ ] ____________________
- [ ] ____________________

THINGS THAT YOU DO BEST *(great writer; good with people; computer skills etc.)*

____

____

____

____

____

Designed by Jamal Harley 6/19/2012

But he also gave students tools he thought might be helpful, such as the Weekly Time Budget sheet (see page 5). Other planning documents that helped Ervin Scholars get organized are the John B. Ervin Scholars Program Semester Goals and Long Term Planner.

Long Term Planner

Week of	Sunday	Monday	Tuesday	Wednesday	Thursday	Friday	Saturday
Aug. 26			Classes Begin				
Sept. 2		Labor Day					
Sept. 9							
Sept. 16							
Sept. 23							
Sept. 30							
Oct. 7							
Oct. 14						Fall Break	
Oct. 21							
Oct. 28							
Nov. 4							
Nov. 11							
Nov. 18				Thanksgiving Break	Thanksgiving Break	Thanksgiving Break	
Nov. 25							
Dec. 2							
Dec. 9					Final Exams Begin		
Dec. 16				Final Exams End	Winter Break Begins		

*Use this sheet to fill in important due dates for papers and projects, in addition to your exams, so that all of that information is available to you at a quick glance throughout the semester.

ACKNOWLEDGMENTS

Habits of Achievement: Lessons for a Life Well-Lived was initiated by alumni of the Ervin Scholars Program, who cherished the advice that Dean McLeod had given year-by-year at the Ervin Scholars orientation and which had great meaning in their lives. Believing that the "Habits" would be important to all students and alumni, especially those who had the pleasure of knowing James "Jim" McLeod, several alumni formed a committee — chaired by Trina (Williams) Shanks — to work with Margaret West, associate director of the Ervin Scholars Program, to make this book a reality.

Habits of Achievement Book Committee

Trina (Williams) Shanks, *Chair*

Mary Ellen Benson, *Editor*

Danielle Hayes

Matt Holton

Marcy Mamroth, *Graphic Designer*

Clara McLeod

Margaret West

The book committee thanks Chancellor Mark S. Wrighton for his vision, support and encouragement.

The book committee thanks the following for permission to use their quotations in the book:

Charles Brown, Jr.

Solomon Brown

Vincent Caesar

Sacha Coupet

Fernando Cutz

Kim Daily

William H. Danforth

Bailey Davidson

Gerald Early

Amy Fletcher

Regina Frey

Kelley Greenman

Michele Hall

Matt Holton

Aaron Hutcherson

Shaun Koiner

Barry L. Levy

Mackenzie (Leonard) Lober

Edward S. Macias

Anthony Maltbia

Nadia Mann

Clara McLeod

Jeff McLeod

Keri McWilliams

Amoretta Morris

Christopher Murriel

Chrystal Okonta

N'Jai-An Patters

Michelle Purdy

Allory Relf

Richard A. Roloff

Egon Schwarz

Trina (Williams) Shanks

Eboni Sharp

Kimberly Short

Ed Stowe

Jerome Strickland

Tim Taylor

Lynnell Thomas

Robert L. Virgil

Gregg Walker

Mark S. Wrighton

The committee especially thanks Chancellor Mark S. Wrighton, Chancellor Emeritus William H. Danforth, and Wayne Fields, the Lynne Cooper Harvey Distinguished Professor of English for the Foreword, Introduction, and Afterword, respectively.

The committee thanks Candace O'Connor for her sage advice and editorial input.

The committee thanks Rudolph Clay, Olin Library Outreach Services, for assistance with obtaining permission to use quotes.

The remarks by Gerald Early, the Merle Kling Professor of Modern Letters, on pages 56-57 are an excerpt from "The Parable of the Fox and the Hedgehog" address given at the unveiling of the James E. McLeod portrait in May 2010 and are used with permission from Gerald Early.

The illustration by Steve Edwards on page 60, "Jim McLeod 25th year," is used with permission from Steve Edwards.

The Afterword by Wayne Fields, "Arts and Sciences Recognition Ceremony — Commencement 2012," May 17, 2012, is used with permission from Wayne Fields.

The John Wesley quote on page 34 comes from *Letters of John Wesley.* (Hodder and Stoughton: 1915)

Grateful acknowledgment is made to the following for their assistance with photographs:

The McLeod family

Rudolph Clay, Olin Library Outreach Services

Sonya Rooney and Miranda Rectenwald, Washington University Archives

Joe Angeles and Elaine Pittaluga, WUSTL Photos

Grateful acknowledgment is made to the following for permission to reprint previously published material:

The quotation from Alfred Binet on page 2, *Les idées modernes sur les enfants* (Paris, E. Flammarion, 1909), translated from the French by Suzanne Heisler, *Modern Ideas about Children* (Menlo Park, CA, pages 106–107, © 1975 Suzanne Heisler), is used with permission from Suzanne Heisler Speece and her husband, Ralph Speece.

Dover Publications, Inc.: The quote on page 30 is from William James, *The Principles of Psychology*, Vol. 1, pp. 403–404 and is used with permission from Dover Publications.

Madeline Drexler: The excerpt by Madeline Drexler on page 28, copyright © by Madeline Drexler, is reprinted with permission of the author.

The quotation on page 32, from *Positivity: Groundbreaking research reveals how to embrace the hidden strength of positive emotions, overcome negativity, and thrive,* copyright © 2009 by Barbara Fredrickson, is reprinted with permission of the author.

International Bible Society: Ecclesiastes 3 (page 31) Scripture taken from the HOLY BIBLE, NEW INTERNATIONAL VERSION®. Copyright © 1973, 1978, 1984 by International Bible Society. Used by permission of Zondervan Publishing House. All rights reserved.

The "NIV" and "New International Version" trademarks are registered in the United States Patent and Trademark Office by International Bible Society. Use of either trademark requires the permission of International Bible Society.

Keare family: Miriam Hamilton Keare's "Golden Rules for Living" (page 14) is reprinted with permission from her family.

Anne Lamott: The excerpt from *Bird by Bird: Some Instructions on Writing and Life,* on page 3, copyright © Anne Lamott 1994 is reprinted with permission from Anne Lamott.

Nelson Mandela Centre of Memory: The excerpt on page 36, from Nelson Mandela's Statement from the Dock at the Opening of the Defence Case in the Rivonia Trial, Pretoria Supreme Court, South Africa, 20th April 1964, is used with permission from the Nelson Mandela Centre of Memory.

Frank L. Outlaw: The quote on page 9, written by Frank L. Outlaw, the late president of BI-LO Stores, is used with permission from his son, Frank Outlaw.

BIBLIOGRAPHY

The quotations that appear in this book come from a variety of sources. Some come from notes, emails and Facebook postings to the Ervin Scholars Program office. Others come from personal notes written to the McLeod family at the time of the McLeod Scholars Program reception on May 6, 2010, and at the James E. McLeod memorial service on October 9, 2011. Still others come from published accounts in places like *Washington Magazine* and the *St. Louis American* newspaper. And some of the quotations were written specifically for this book.

A partial list of sources follows.

Partial Bibliography

American staff, "Ronald Herd II honors Dean James E. McLeod and Dr. John B. Ervin," *St. Louis American*, February 16, 2012

"Brookings Quadrangle bench to be dedicated for Jim McLeod Sept. 16," August 31, 2012, https://news.wustl.edu/news/Pages/24186.aspx

William H. Danforth, Remarks at the James E. McLeod Memorial Service, October 9, 2011, http://www.youtube.com/watch?v=g8h5xmaENzU&feature=relmfu

Gerald Early, "The Parable of the Fox and the Hedgehog," Remarks at the McLeod Scholars Program reception and unveiling of the James E. McLeod portrait, May 6, 2010

"Ervin Scholars celebrate and reflect on program's past 25 years," September 25, 2012, https://news.wustl.edu/news/Pages/24298.aspx

"John B. Ervin Scholars Program," recruitment brochure, (Washington University, 2011)

Wayne Fields, Remarks at Arts & Sciences Recognition Ceremony — Commencement 2012, May 17, 2012

"Jim McLeod's 'special way' to be remembered with special place on South 40," August 20, 2012, http://news.wustl.edu/news/Pages/24114.aspx

Shaun Koiner, Remarks at the McLeod's Way dedication, September 15, 2012 (unpublished manuscript)

Barry L. Levy, Letter to James E. McLeod Scholarship, December 31, 2009 (unpublished)

Monica C. Lewis, "Part I: A Legacy of Excellence," *Legacies: A History of the John B. Ervin Scholars Program at Washington University in St. Louis*, (Washington University, 2001 and 2007)

Joanna Luo, "'McLeod's Way' cemented," *Student Life*, September 17, 2012, www.studlife.com/news/campus-events/2012/0917/mcleods-way-cemented/print/

Edward S. Macias, Remarks at the James E. McLeod Memorial Service, October 9, 2011, http://www.youtube.com/watch?v=ULLVy18Qwa8&feature=relmfu

Susan Killenberg McGinn, "Ervin Scholars Program celebrates 25 years," September 12, 2012, http://news.wustl.edu/news/Pages/24229.aspx

Susan Killenberg McGinn, "James E. McLeod, 67," September 7, 2011, http://news.wustl.edu/news/Pages/22644.aspx

Susan Killenberg McGinn, "Remembering James E. McLeod," *St. Louis American*, September 15, 2011

Clara P. McLeod, Remarks at the McLeod's Way dedication, September 15, 2012 (unpublished manuscript)

James E. McLeod, Remarks on receiving the St. Louis American Foundation's Salute to Excellence in Education Lifetime Achievement Award, 2008 (unpublished manuscript)

Jeff McLeod, Remarks at the James E. McLeod Memorial Service, October 9, 2011, http://www.youtube.com/watch?v=wkgw8vDijMc&feature=relmfu

Carol Moakley, Interview with Jim McLeod, October 5, 2007 (unpublished manuscript)

Candace O'Connor, Jim McLeod Interview, April 2011 (unpublished manuscript)

Candace O'Connor, "A Guiding Hand," *Washington Magazine*, February 2012, http://magazine.wustl.edu/2012/February/Pages/DeanMcLeodGuidingHand.aspx

Candace O'Connor, "Guiding the Student Experience," *Washington Magazine*, Fall 2001, magazine-archives.wustl.edu/Fall01/washingtonspirit.html

Michelle A. Purdy, "Part II: A Legacy of Commitment," *Legacies: A History of the John B. Ervin Scholars Program at Washington University in St. Louis*, (Washington University, 2007)

Rebecca S. Rivas, "Jim McLeod, pioneering Washington University dean, passes at 67," *St. Louis American*, September 8, 2011

Gloria S. Ross, "James Earl McLeod: Revered Washington University dean," *St. Louis Beacon*, September 7, 2011

Robert L. Virgil, Remarks at the James E. McLeod Memorial Service, October 9, 2011, http://www.youtube.com/watch?v=XqFBE7_KBIE&feature=relmfu

Mark S. Wrighton, Remarks at the James E. McLeod Memorial Service, October 9, 2011, http://www.youtube.com/watch?v=PATWdlq85X0&feature=relmfu

Habits of Achievement: Lessons for a Life Well-Lived

Spring 2013
Fonts: Minion Pro, Trade Gothic, Bodoni Ornaments ITC
Cover: Sterling Cover C1S
Endleaf: French/Construction/Electric Red/80# Cover/30% Post Consumer Waste
Paper: McCoy Silk/Ultra Blue White/Dull/80# Text/10% Post Consumer Waste
Printer: Columbine Printing Company
Place of publication: St. Louis, Missouri
Printed in an edition of 4,000

Back cover photo by Herb Weitman